His Love Is Not Blind

by
Mike Haywood

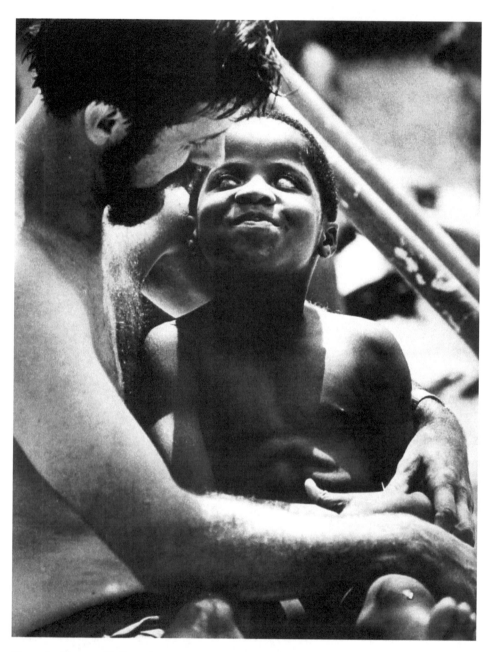

Photo by Everett Hullum for *MissionsUSA*, an SBC publication

His Love Is Not Blind

Recollections of the Peninsula Baptist Association's Camps for the Deaf & Blind

by

Mike Haywood

Map of Piankatank by Jim Ailor

ISBN 978-1-716-49221-1

Table of Contents

Dedication

This book is dedicated to those who are not mentioned, or who are mentioned only in passing. It was you who came to our retreats and other events and simply shared your life and love. You did not make a funny mistake or have an unusual situation happen to you (at least as far as I was aware). But you made things special. You reflected the love of Jesus Christ. You made this a ministry. And if some neat things happened to you that are not recorded here, that is OK. Because, as my pastor and friend Chester Brown once said, "It's OK if we forget the good things, because God will always remember." Thanks for being my friends. And thanks for your ministry to some pretty special people.

> God bless, and keep smiling.
> Mike Haywood
> (Matthew 19:30)

Map of Camp Piankatank

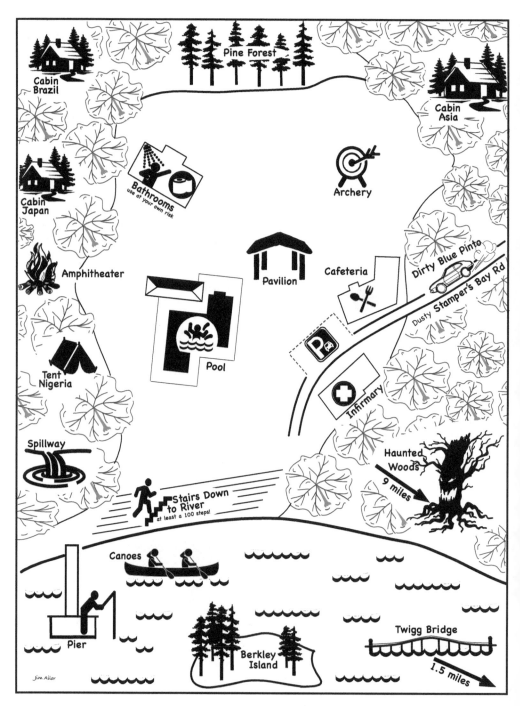

1

Craig Waddell

Craig Waddell was known as the *punster*—he still is, even today. Not a *punter*, a punster, although he was also a football player. More importantly, Craig was very creative. At various times, we all had to admit, we appreciated the boy's characteristics. It was nice to have him working for me during the summers, and it was definitely nice to have him on my side.

I first met Craig when he was in middle school. His dad, Jack, was the pastor of one of our local churches and a friend of mine. At some point, Jack wanted me to get to know Craig (or perhaps it was the other way around). We got together at times after school for soda and coffee. (I usually have a great memory for trivial things, but I can't remember if Craig, who is now as big a coffee drinker as myself, was drinking coffee or soda during those meetings.) I wisely decided that this big, muscular kid was pretty sharp and would fit in perfectly with our merry band of volunteers. After I heard his first nine or ten puns, I knew he was my kind of teen. Since the day I first met Craig, he has been a good friend.

That ability to do what is necessary, to cut through the knots of a problem, was a must in the line of ministry I would be doing with Craig. Luckily, I had him and a good group of teens who could do just that. Dealing with the unexpected was the name of the game when working with the hearing and visually impaired young. Actually, most of the problems we encountered had nothing to do with the kids themselves.

At that time, we collaborated a lot with two of our state institutions. One, the state Rehabilitation Center for the Blind, is located in Richmond. They run a year-round program with dorms for the trainees. One can go here to learn everything, from using a cane to making crafts, from sewing to banking, from Braille to computers. We worked with several absolutely wonderful workers from the rehabilitation center, including Rosetta Robinson and Gail Pearsall.

The second institution was located in our area. It was one of the two state schools for the hearing and visually impaired, as well as the multi-handicapped. They also ran special summer courses for their students. The school included grades one through twelve, whereas the center in Richmond is open to people of any age. (Several years ago, the state decided to consolidate the two schools, and unfortunately the Hampton school was closed.)

Each agency would send a number of students on our summer retreats. Over the years, we added many other events for them, but in the early days we started with the summer retreats. The staff at both agencies were super with their clients. There were a few exceptions, of course.
One year, two workers from the Hampton school wanted to come on the retreat. They stayed for all of one hour. Next thing I knew, they had packed and gone, without telling me. Their complaints being that (1) they had to stay in cabins with the students, and (2) the bathrooms had no shower curtains. Good thing they didn't stay long enough to see the bugs! But again, I need to emphasize that they were the exception.

Speaking of bugs reminds me of something that happened many years later when I had two Latvian girls working for me during the summer. This was the same summer that Craig brought over a contingent of Austrian and Romanian youth. Anyway, I took Liga and Ieva with me to the GA state camp in the mountains. It turned out to be the wettest week of the summer, and as a result, there were more than the usual number of bugs infesting the cabins.

Susie Wright, one of my previous summer workers, was on the GA camp staff that year, and she enabled my two young friends to be junior counselors for the week. The morning after their first night at the camp, Susie caught up with me and related the following story. In fairness, it should be said that there were some really big bugs in the cabin that night.

4

Evidently, the two girls wanted no part of any bugs, and they took the following precaution: After making their bunks and unrolling their sleeping bags for the night, they sprayed a circle on the floor around their bunks with OFF. Then, simultaneously, like Edrick and Howard diving into the pool (you will meet them soon), they leapt over the circle and into their sleeping bags, pulling them over their heads.

The next morning, Liga came to me at breakfast, looked me square in the eye, and stated, "I hate you!" Ieva came up behind her and called me "Big Bug." Unfortunately, that name stuck for a good while. It turned out that they do not have big bugs in Riga, Latvia, and this had been quite a shock. I told them they had better get used to the bugs at this camp because they would see the really big bugs when they got to Piankatank.

Anyway, all of this is to explain that, like any state institution, we learned to live with the fact that some bureaucratic foul-ups would inevitably occur from time to time. Those could be real problems, and they were often tied to transportation issues. We tried to always have an alternate plan.

Craig Waddell takes advantage of whatever is around to give campers a new experience.

Above: Wendy Remey with one of the Virginia School's state-ranked wrestlers

Below: Lori Blankenship with friends—three beautiful smiles

2

Transportation

*C*raig later told me that he thought I must have been mildly prophetic in sending him out to the school one Friday. A group from the School for the Deaf and Blind was supposed to meet the rest of us at my office that afternoon. The school had promised to transport the kids to camp in one of the state vans.

Teachers Dean Jernigan and Larry van Wyngarden were coming along. These two didn't care about shower curtains or having to sleep in the same cabin with the kids. They were two of the best teachers at the school and could always be counted on to enhance the camp. (Several years later, I would work with the school's coach, Dennis Ruffin. Dennis was another fantastic individual, and we teamed up on activities at the school gym for twenty-five years.)

A state van was essential because Dean was on a medication that, according to his doctor, made it inadvisable for him to drive. Larry would take some of the kids in his car, but the rest, and all the luggage, would go into the van. The school administration had promised a driver for the weekend.

I had played this game with the school personnel before (not with Dean or Larry), and so I asked Craig if he would go out there, just in case. Craig was driving his dad's old car, which could carry quite a load. Early that Friday afternoon, he pulled off the main road that ran in front of the school and proceeded to drive through the big entrance gate. The road into the school ended at a tee. There, as expected, was a group of high-school kids milling around. It turned out to be the only thing that went according to plan at the school that day!

The students were ready for the weekend, suitcases standing at the curb. Each of them was wearing sunglasses and had the ever-present ghetto blaster perched on their shoulders. Their eyes might have been sensitive to bright sunlight, but there was not a thing wrong with the rest of their bodies. This year's group included some of the top wrestlers in the state, among sighted and unsighted students.

Dean and Larry were obviously at home among the kids. Both long-time teachers, they were the kind of people who gave a lot of extra time to help their students. They were also involved, along with Bob Moore, in one of the local Exchange Clubs. It was kind of neat that I got to know Bob Moore through a scuba diving club and the other two guys through my ministry. Then, on the first overnight camp, we all came together.

The Exchange Club had been helping me out for many years, giving money toward our retreats and other events with the visually impaired. Several years earlier, when I was working for the Welfare Department, three high-school seniors, whose mothers were on welfare, were graduating. The families did not have the money to spend on class rings, and so I got in touch with Bob Moore. All three got their rings, courtesy of the Wythe Exchange Club. (The other nice thing about the club was that they always invited me to a free meal whenever they were going to present me with a check.)

Craig maneuvered through a crowd of cheerful voices and smiles, parking his car next to the two teachers. As they stepped to the car, the contrast of their expressions as opposed to the students' glee told Craig that something was amiss. Before they said a word, Craig realized the problem. There was no van. For some reason, he was not the least bit surprised.

Clearly exasperated, Dean said, "Someone sent the van out to be serviced. They didn't even bother to check the sign-out sheet. And to top that off, the driver didn't show. So, we don't even have a driver for the van we don't have!"

Larry smiled and continued the one-way conversation. "You're a sight for sore eyes—excuse the pun. Dean can't drive because of the medication he's taking. I can get some of the group in my car. We were thinking we would have to make two trips to Haywood's office."

"No problem," said Craig. "We can pack my car."

"Well," Dean said, "perhaps there is one problem, but we can take care of that. I can't drive, and although you'll do fine, it's against regulations for a non-staff member to drive the kids. Just in case someone is watching, Larry will need to drive your car off the school grounds. Then you can take over, and Larry will walk back to his car. Is that OK with you?"

Craig said again, "No problem. Let's get loaded."

Students turned off their blasters, grabbed some luggage, and helped each other move toward the cars. Some of the partially sighted helped the totally blind to find their way. Craig watched a train comprised of one partially sighted young man leading three of his friends, each holding onto the elbow of the person in front. They slowly snaked their way to the back door of the wagon. A few with canes walked by themselves, guided by the sounds of laughter and directions shouted by friends. This was one of the things that always impressed us. The vision-impaired students used the abilities they possessed to help each other cope with whatever situations they faced. Usually, such assistance came with a lot of laughter and encouragement.

Craig, Larry, and Dean helped the students into the cars. Thus, they were able to head out, leaving none behind, all in one trip. Twenty minutes later they pulled into the parking lot of the Peninsula Baptist Association (PBA).

Andrea with Edrick and Howard (Ronnie to the right)

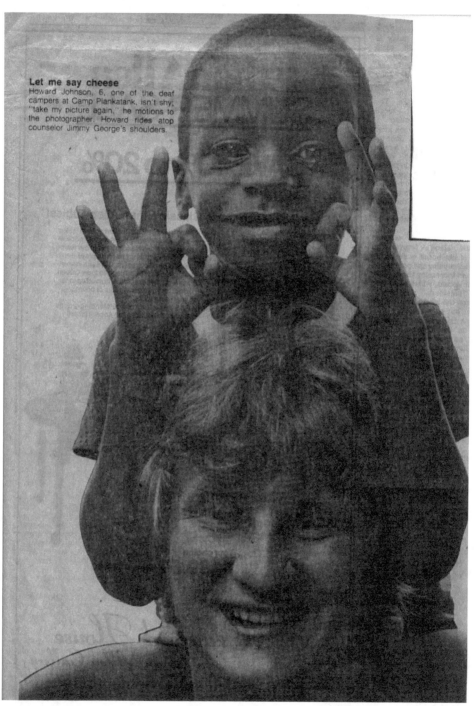

Let me say cheese
Howard Johnson, 6, one of the deaf campers at Camp Plankatank, isn't shy; "take my picture again," he motions to the photographer. Howard rides atop counselor Jimmy George's shoulders.

From the August 9, 1980, article by Betsy Raper in the *Daily Press*; photo by Michael Dillard

3
The Parking Lot

One of the high points of each year's retreat was the parking lot of the Peninsula Baptist Association. Many of the volunteers had not seen each other in a while, and in our early days, we saw very little of our hearing-impaired friends during the year. The office parking lot was an annual beehive of activity with cars dropping people off, both campers and volunteers.

Close to sixty would congregate here before the hour-long ride to camp. Understandably, the parking lot was a madhouse, with both voices and flying fingers, signing at full speed as friends caught up on the latest. We would pick up a few more at various spots along the way, and by the time we made it to camp, our number swelled to around a hundred.

At some point during the early afternoon, an event we all had been anticipating occurred. One specific car pulled into the parking lot, and all the action froze. Both back doors simultaneously opened and out jumped two five-year-old boys, inseparable friends. They would spend the entire weekend in a state of perpetual motion, most of it perfectly synchronized. This dynamic duo was Howard and Edrick.

Each wore a smile that stayed on their faces from Friday afternoon until Sunday evening. We used to fight over who would get to work with them. They had come on their first retreat the year before. Like then, they showed up ready and set to hit the water as soon as they got to camp…perhaps before. There is a lake behind the PBA office building, and they are the only two kids I ever truly worried about jumping in for a swim. Other necessities might be forgotten, but they carried with them their towels, floats, and diving masks. I have never met any two kids who loved the water as much as Edrick and Howard.

Last year, their counselors observed the same routine each morning. Howard and Edrick would wake up long before the alarm. (The alarm was for the counselors and obviously not for these two—and not just because they were hearing impaired.) After grinning at each other, they would look around at their snoozing bunkmates. The counselors were generally awake by that time, but they were adept at appearing to sleep until the alarm went off. Every moment in the sack was heavily guarded. The two campers would sit in their beds, signing to each other and patiently waiting until someone finally opened their eyes. Then they would jump out of bed at the same time, make swimming motions with their arms, and ask in sign language what time the pool opened.

That first year, they also gave us a classic example of complete trust. In doing so, they proved my own trust in my young counselors. Although both of the boys loved the water, and a year later became excellent swimmers, that first year they could not swim a lick. For these two, however, a lack of swimming ability was not going to deter them from having fun in the pool. They quickly became attached to their counselors and made them a part of their favorite pool game, which went as follows.

Howard and Edrick would grab their counselors and point away from the pool. Once the volunteers learned how the game was to be played, they would obediently turn and look in the direction the boys pointed. The two friends shared that special mental wavelength, which allowed them to do this simultaneously. As soon as the counselors' heads were turned, Edrick and Howard would jump into the pool.

The counselors would turn back in time to see two splashes. I should point out that the major part of these retreats centered around water sports. Probably a quarter of my counselors were trained lifeguards. At the pool, we always had three or four lifeguards on duty. Therefore, there was no danger in this game. But, as I said, at the time, the boys could not swim. All they could do was lie in the water and wait for their counselors to jump in and pull them out. And, of course, that was exactly what happened. When pulled up, there would be big grins on their faces, and they would gesture to be taken to the poolside, where they could repeat the whole process.

During the course of that retreat, we had alternated between playing the game and making them work on swimming strokes. By the end of the retreat, they were making a little progress. This second summer, we were in for a special treat. Their parents told us that both boys had taken lessons and were getting to be good swimmers. Eventually, they became very skilled in the water. That game, played on their first retreat with us, is one of the best examples of complete trust in a friend that I have ever witnessed.

We kept a close watch on the two as they spun around the parking lot. As I mentioned before, I didn't know how much of a temptation the lake out back would be. For the time being, they were running from one volunteer to another, asking what time we would be going swimming this afternoon.

Howard's mom called me over and told me another interesting story about the boys. Last year, she and Edrick's mom had made the mistake of telling their sons about the retreat on the Monday before. It had taken them all of five minutes to get psyched. Then, as Howard's mom related, every hour on the hour, for five days, they would ask, "Is it time to go to camp yet?" The guys were pumped. This year, they were not told which weekend the retreat was until lunch that very day. Thus, the ladies only had to answer the question three or four times.

In the early nineties, we held a reunion for the camp staff. A good number were able to attend, although several could not get back to town, including Jeri Hudson Wickiser. Jeri sent a letter, which included the following comments:

I wish I could be there to experience it all [the reunion].... Does Steve Skinner still have his leather hat and Alice? Is it true Jimmy George is preaching...the same Jimmy George who told Marianne and me that we didn't need a devotion every night: "Don't get too religious on me!"? I wonder if Marianne has kids who like to sing into the electric fans...just the way Marianne and I would to entertain ourselves. And yes, Steve and Jimmy, I still say, "Be careful or you'll poke someone's eye out!" — a phrase which gave them a lot of laughs. Have a great time!

—Jeri

Truth be known, we were all pumped for this particular event, and no one more so than the volunteers. We did a lot of different ministries over the course of the year, including other retreats, but this one seemed to have a special flavor. As a result, I had no trouble getting all the help I needed. In fact, generally I had to turn down a bunch of would-be counselors—good ones at that. I was so besieged with offers of help that I had to make a rule that a volunteer had to participate in some other ministry before being qualified to attend this retreat.

There always seemed to be something magical about it. Perhaps that was due in part to the fact that it was the first thing we ever did with a group of vision-impaired students. Even the way it got started was unique. We began this ministry because of racial prejudice. I guess it shows that the Lord can truly use any situation to reach out to others. It got started a few years before I went to work at the Peninsula Baptist Association, when I was a caseworker for the Hampton Department of Social Services.

Nancy Hayes and Edrick

4
The Nude in the Living Room

During my two years as a protective services officer for the Welfare Department, we faced one never-ending problem—a lack of emergency foster homes. It was almost a weekly occurrence to go through the following scenario: On Thursday or Friday, one of the workers would run into a situation in which a young person or child needed immediate placement in a foster home. The caseworker would call around and invariably find out that there would be one or two good homes available on Monday. However, finding a place for the young person over the weekend would turn out to be a headache.

To be honest, in such cases we would sometimes end up using a home we had sworn to never use again or find an already overwhelmed foster parent, who would take in one more child for the weekend. In addition, we would often run into a situation in which a young person needed to be out of their home for only a few days or perhaps a week. Since long-term homes were hard to find, it seemed the department used most of its time performing case studies on homes for long-term placement. Thus, there were almost no emergency, short-term homes to be found.

Therefore, when I left for the PBA, my fellow workers sent me off with a party, a gift, and a request to come up with some good Baptist emergency homes. I think that is when I decided that my motto would be "Sure, no sweat! We'll do it. I don't have a clue how, but we will get it done!" It worked perfectly, and for eight years many of our church families were able to provide loving homes for some very special children and teens.

Later, I worked with other community leaders to set up our area's first group foster home. Others followed, and eventually our ministry was no longer needed. That was OK, because in the meantime, other needs had come to our attention. Some of my homes eventually became long-term foster homes through the Social Service Department, and one or two became adoptive parents. The far majority, however, were a short-term beacon of light, shining in the night for a specific child of God.

After the first two years, word got around about this ministry, and from time to time, we would get calls from other agencies, asking if we could provide space for one of their clients. Then, sometime in 1972, I got a call from the social worker at the Virginia School for the Deaf, Blind, and Multi-disabled. (The full name was a mouthful. Their correspondence often just said "Virginia School at Hampton.") She told me she had a problem that she hoped the PBA could help out with.

I was not at all familiar with the school at the time. Mary Ann Shiloh gave me a little general background and told me about the summer program that the school ran. It was a ten-week enrichment program for vision-impaired high-school students. The program was set up to put these students in situations where they would have to interact with the general public. They would do such things as go shopping at the mall, eat out at restaurants, and visit museums. She went on to say that they took students from all over the state. The students would stay in the school dorms for the ten weeks. This was the cause of her dilemma. The dorms, of course, were integrated. Because of that, the parents of two white teenage girls were refusing to let their daughters attend the summer session.

Mary Ann disagreed with the parents' view, but she did not want the girls to miss out on the experience. Rather than make an issue of the point, she was looking for a place where the two girls could stay for the summer. Her big question was whether I could find one or two homes that would take them in for the ten weeks. The state would pay for room and board. I told Mary Ann I did not think we would have any problem. I was right. In fact, things went so smoothly, they came back the next year under the same arrangements.

Like myself, my foster parents had no past acquaintance with vision-impaired youth. What they learned very quickly was that all of us are pretty much the same and that we need to relate to all people in a normal manner. (Because I was busy with other things that summer, I did not get to spend much time with the host families. Therefore, my foster parents learned this lesson much sooner than I. However, my education was not far behind.)

The two girls were very personable, and my families had almost no problems in accepting them into their homes as part of the family. Still, anytime you're dealing with people, the unexpected can and usually will happen. The first week, a rather humorous incident took place. Mrs. Haynes, one of my foster mothers, lived in a house with a large picture window in the living room. It gave a great view of a busy side street. Of course, the window gave anyone walking or driving down the street an open view of the living room. This was fine with Mrs. Haynes, or at least it was, until one Saturday morning when she was watching TV. This was about three days after her summer daughter had come to stay.

She heard the bathroom door open and then watched in amazement as a totally nude young lady calmly walked through the living room. As far as I can remember, there were no traffic accidents that morning. Somewhat stunned, Mrs. Haynes continued to watch as her new foster daughter went to the ice box and pulled out a Coke. By the time she had opened the soft drink, the window blinds were down and closed.

It turned out that this seventeen-year-old and her mother lived in a farmhouse out in the middle of nowhere. There was no one around, and there were no picture windows in the house. At home, if she got out of the shower and decided she needed something from another room, she would not bother to stop and dress until she got back to her bedroom. Luckily, this was one of those problems, while not easily foreseen, that is easily remedied. It did provide a lot of laughter for both of them after Mrs. Haynes explained the issue. A few words of explanation, and all was fine. I kind of think the blinds did stay closed for a few days, just to make sure.

In talking with Mary Ann about their summer program, I found out that, while they did quite a bit with the students, they had not been able to offer anything of a camping nature. Mary Ann told me they didn't have the volunteers needed for such a venture. My mind immediately went *click!* I like to do outdoor things, and I knew a lot of young people in our churches who could help out in a camp setting.

In fact, that had been one of the first things I did after coming to the

PBA. The first two summers, we held camping retreats for kids on probation. They had gone very well, so now I figured, why not camp with the visually impaired? I mentioned it to Mary Ann, and she jumped at the idea.

For the next two summers, we organized a one-day outing with the vision-impaired students. Jim Ailor and Jay Lawson helped with both, which we held at our association camp, Eastover. Then, we expanded to an overnight retreat, followed the next year by a two-nighter. Soon, we progressed to a pair of summer retreats, which were held for both vision- and hearing-impaired youth.

The very first camp that I ran at Piankatank was for youth on probation from the three cities in our area. The camp was great, and the probation officers who helped out gave us good reviews. I ran into a few snags but learned a lot.

Jim Ailor was on that retreat, and among other things, he held a worship service at the waterfront. (Jim was not on probation, though some people at his local church felt he might should have been!) It was meaningful, with only one minor incident. Jim, as anyone who knows him will attest, tends to approach things in a different manner. He definitely likes to get outside the box. Anyway, his sermon was on Old Testament prophets. Because many of them lived a bit out of the box themselves, Jim called his sermon "Bible Weirdos."

After the sermon, one of the campers came up to me and said, "He should never call someone in the Bible a *weirdo!*" The camper was pretty upset, but I was diplomatic and didn't ask if he had actually read that much in the Old Testament. I said he had a point and left it at that.

It was during those first two years that my volunteers and I learned what my foster parents had already experienced. The Lord often uses humorous comments and events to teach us serious lessons. Never has that been truer than in this ministry. One of the more interesting aspects of life with my friends and volunteers is the number of one-liners we can come up with. Many have come from the vision-impaired students. For if their sight is dark, their sense of humor is very bright. In fact, probably the whole tempo of our relationship with this group of new friends was set with a single remark made on our first trip, which you will hear about in the next chapter.

Actually, I did not run the first outing with the visually impaired. I made the commitment and a few of the preliminary plans. Then I left the PBA for a year or so. My replacement, Jean Rozema (a super person), had to do the first one. She asked me to come on that trip as a volunteer, but it was Jean who initiated this great ministry. The first, a day trip, was held at Eastover in Surry County. We returned there my first year back, and then the next year, we moved to Camp Piankatank and overnights.

Jim Ailor helps a camper with her talent, involving a phone conversation.

Above: Stel, Bill, and Jimmy sing at the talent show.

Below: Chuck Paul, Cliff Bowen, and others eat in the cafeteria.

5
Stel's Dates

At the time, we were not sure how our vision-impaired campers would react to comments that made reference to sight. I can vividly remember preparing with my helpers the week before our first outing. Every time we got together, someone would mention that they were really afraid of offending one of the campers with a chance remark. We thought it would be terrible to mention sight to people who didn't have it.

Do you see my point? (Sorry. I couldn't resist.) That is exactly the kind of thing we were afraid of saying. Of course, the truth is that the visually impaired use the same idioms we do, even the ones referring to sight. We had just not learned that yet.

So it was that my very good friend Stel Washburn was walking with two teenage boys on a lazy, sun-filled morning at Camp Piankatank. Both the boys were totally blind. Either because she had not yet learned the correct method as a sighted guide (hand to elbow), or just because it was a nice morning to be strolling with newfound friends, Stel was linked arm in arm with both guys, heading for the cafeteria. It was lunch time at good ole Camp Piankatank.

The cafeteria was an old building, which also served as the activities and recreation center. At the retreat, you could eat all you wanted and still not put on weight. I'm not sure that the daytime temperature in the cafeteria ever dropped below ninety-five degrees. Each mealtime, you could count on sweating off as many calories as you took in.

That is, if you ate the meals. Truthfully, I always liked the food and would look forward to going back for seconds. However, I think many of the volunteers would take issue with that last statement. I think they were just finicky eaters. One legitimate complaint was my fault. The cooks made what I thought was a great beef stew. I would request it for the last meal of the weekend no matter how hot it was. Since the mid-day temperature in the dining hall usually hovered around 98.7, it was probably not the best thing to serve. Too bad! I always enjoyed it.

Regardless, it is necessary to keep up one's strength, and thus Stel and her two beaus were on their way to eat. Being nice and keeping up conversation, Stel remarked that she felt like a high-school girl going to her junior prom.

One of the guys replied, "Right, and we are your blind dates!"

Stel laughed and kept on walking. Still, she was aware that she had learned a very valuable lesson, and she was quick to share that insight with the rest of us. From that point on, we all had a new respect for our sightless friends. We learned to do what my foster parents had—just relax and be yourself. The visually impaired are exactly like the rest of us in all areas of life, even in humor. It's just that they don't see so well.

That retreat, or perhaps the next, my education continued. We were at Piankatank, and one of the partially sighted fellows, named Sam, had come up to me two or three times to say that he needed to go to the bathroom. Each time, I would let him take me by the elbow (I was proud to know the correct method of being a sighted guide), and I proceeded to the restroom. Don Meekens, who worked with the school at the time, was with us on this one. Once again, Sam told me he needed to go. I started to take him when Don spoke up and told me that Sam was a partial and didn't need any help finding the restroom. He was just letting me know where he was going!

OK, so it took me a while to figure all this out. I did finally learn a valuable lesson, which I have tried to keep with me: **All of us have areas of ability and limitation. It is just that some limitations have labels placed on them, like "vision- or hearing-impaired." The rest of us have limitations, which are very real but not categorized. We need to be sure and look for the abilities in others and not let their limitations get in the way of our relationship with them. We also do not need to always be "doing for" the person with disabilities.**

The following joke was told to me by a totally blind young man: There was a boy and girl who were dating. Both of them were blind. The boy got word that his girlfriend was running around on him. He caught up with her one day and confronted her. When she heard the accusations, she immediately denied them, insisting that she was completely true. "OK," he said, as he popped out one of his false eyes and placed it on top of her head. "But just remember—I'm keeping my eye on you!"

Above: Stel playing Siamese softball

Right: Campers with smiles

Above: Mary Elizabeth Brown and her new friend head for their cabin.

Below: Waylon with Susan Williams, Karen Watts, and Julie Knowles

6
Parking Lot Revisited

I know it was a little out of character for me to veer off subject, but I was talking about the parking lot, wasn't I? When we left the parking lot for my reminiscence (thank goodness for spellcheck), Howard and Edrick were weaving in and out of everything and everybody in the lot. (OK, most of my counselors would tell you that I am always getting off subject!)

Parents exchanged a few words of greeting to each other and some of the volunteers and double-checked about what time to be back on Sunday. Then, with big smiles, they departed for what was hopefully going to be a quiet weekend. (They deserved it, too. These are among some of the most patient parents in the world.)

We still had a few more people, both volunteers and campers, to add to our merry band as we made our way to camp. Upon arrival, we would meet up with the group of campers from the state Rehabilitation Center for the Blind. (Other than the Campus Life van, our only mode of transportation was our counselors' cars. During that period, Ike Newingham and his van was a lifesaver in the transportation department, over and over and over again. Later, the Peninsula Baptist purchased two vans.)

After a word of welcome to all and a much-needed prayer, we packed up the vehicles. Actually, I shouldn't gloss over the departing prayer. My crew of volunteers knew that lots of prayer was essential for survival. (Not because of the campers, but because of ourselves.) After loading the cars, we would inevitably hear the repeated chorus, "I have to use the bathroom!" So, we unloaded the cars and unlocked the door to the office, so the *volunteers* could use the potty. Sometimes, one of two of the campers would also need the restrooms, but it was generally the workers.

During those days, the road to Piankatank ran through the parking lot (we were big on parking lots) of the Gloucester McDonald's. There, we would hook up with the Williamsburg girls (Becky Russell and Stella Totty) and two more hearing-impaired boys.

This particular year, I needed to make a special run to pick up a very sweet hearing-impaired girl named Tammi. Because of home problems, Tammi had been committed to a psychiatric unit at a local hospital. We had gotten special permission for her to spend the weekend with us. She had gone with us the year before and was another favorite of my helpers. I signed Tammi out and headed for the McDonald's, where we caught up with the rest of the gang.

Tammi had fair use of her voice. Among our hearing-impaired friends (and the general hearing-impaired population), there was a wide range of ability in this regard. Tammi was better than a lot. Many would not use any "voice" until they knew you well and knew you would not make fun of them.

When I first got involved, I got Shannon and several others to play on my women's softball team in the city recreation league. One of the girls, named Tina Trahan, didn't use her voice for several weeks after I met her. The first time I heard her speak was when Tina was at one of our softball practices. I hit her a ground ball that jumped up at the last second and hit her in the mouth. It was not that hard and did no damage, but it did hurt. Tina walked off the field and signed to one of my other players that it hurt her. I walked over with the other player, who was an excellent signer, and told Tina that I knew it hurt her, but she was OK and at some point, needed to go back out to the field. Tina signed to my other player that she was not going back out. I was trying to convince her to return, but she kept refusing. Finally, Tina said the first words I had ever heard her speak, very carefully and emphatically: "I … do … not … want … to … play!"

I signed that I understood and left her with my other player. After a few minutes, Tina let me know that she was ready to head back in. I was really glad because she was one of my better players.

Since Tammi was vocal, she would usually try her jokes on me, and this day was no exception. The thin, long dark-haired girl sitting next to me asked if my socks had any holes in them. I happened to have on a new pair of socks. I told her they had none—yet. "Gee," she said with a smile, "Then how did you get your feet in them?" *Just like my volunteers*, I thought to myself.

Everyone is a comedian. I made a mental note to put her with Craig Waddell.

Our destination was Camp Piankatank, on the shores of the Piankatank River. It is owned by the state Baptist association and is located at the end of a dirt road, which runs off the main route through that area. I was always glad to be in the lead because we created quite a dust storm with a dozen cars stirring things up. Not that it would have made a great deal of difference to my Pinto wagon. It was its usual dirty-blue shade. My car was somewhat legendary for its general dirty exterior, not to mention the abundance of coffee cups and trash piled up on the backseat floor. No one could ever accuse me of littering the streets of my fair city. Still, my email username is *dirtybluepinto.*

I drove by the infirmary on my left and the cafeteria on the opposite side. After passing the cafeteria, I turned into a parking area on the right. There was a large field in front of the parking area, which ran about thirty feet before coming to a pavilion. Behind the pavilion was a wooded area with cabins, large tents on platforms, and a campfire area. To the right of this stand of woods was another open field; it ran behind the cafeteria and led to the archery range.

Hidden in the woods at the back-right side of the archery range was Asia, the most out-of-the-way cabin. It was also the largest cabin at camp, and I usually put a group of older girls in there. (There was always an over-abundance of female volunteers on these events.) They loved being isolated back there—NOT! Being a Baptist camp, the cabins were named for places where we had missionaries. There was one other reason no one liked to draw Asia. It was the farthest cabin from any of the bathrooms. This year the girls were in luck. I was using it as boys' lodging.

Ask any of the old volunteers about the camp and one of the first things they will mention are the bathrooms and shower facilities. The old cabins had no indoor plumbing. One of the bathrooms was located about fifty yards behind the pavilion. There were two others in the opposite direction, on either side of the swimming pool. Neither was what you would call a "high-tech" facility, even for those days.

During the course of the weekend, we would use every bit of the camp property. First, however, we had to get settled into our cabins. We used the pavilion in front of the parking lot as an unloading area. We had a history of running late, and this day was no exception. Therefore, a group of vision-impaired adults was already waiting for us at the shelter. They were from the Richmond rehab center. With them were Gail Pearsall and Rosetta Robinson, craft and recreation specialists at the center. As usual, they had taken bets on just how late we would be.

One of my duties with the PBA was running a youth coed softball league. Somewhere around the eighth or ninth year of doing so, I arrived at the managers' meeting five minutes late. As the meeting started, one of the managers made a motion to commend me for being on time—for he felt five minutes late was the closest I would ever come to being on time!

Left: Gail Pearsall, from the Virginia Rehabilitation Center for the Blind (unfortunately, this is the only picture I have of this remarkable lady)

Below left: Mary Beth Landis

Below right: Becky Russell and Joe Paul

7
Sleeping with Glen?

The first order of business after arriving at camp was to pair up and make cabin assignments. The cabins held twelve to fourteen bunks. We usually put five or six campers in each, with a slightly greater number of counselors. That was because of the unwritten fifty-percent rule, which I'll explain later. For many years, it was actually a lot of fun to call out cabin assignments because, as I said before, no one wanted to get Asia. On the other hand, there were always those who were hoping to be in the same cabin.

I took a lot of kidding over the years about running these retreats without much planning, and in some ways that was true. I did try to leave a lot of room for the volunteers to use their own skills and inter-relational abilities during the weekend. Some of the inter-relational was among the volunteers themselves, but there was also plenty for the campers. However, the counselor/camper match-ups were meticulously planned.

I made the initial match-ups and then revised them several times during the weeks before the retreat. My goal was to bring together counselors and campers who would be of mutual help to each other. The same was true of my goal for each pair of counselors. During the weekend, the buddy counselors would spend a lot of time together and hopefully help each other, learn from one another, and gain a little more insight about themselves in the bargain. They would perhaps even move a bit closer to the person Jesus Christ wanted them to become. Of course, I also tried to make sure I had one experienced volunteer in each pair of helpers. The same detail went into each cabin assignment.

This was going to be the first of a four- to five-year sequence, during which I could be a bit malicious with assignments. As I said, no one really wanted to be in Asia, especially the girls. Then there was the matter of Glen Braxton. At the time, Glen was a good-natured seventeen-year-old, who took a lot of teasing from his fellow students. Glen faced every event in life with a sheepish smile and the fatalistic outlook that, if anything embarrassing were to happen, it would probably happen to him.

One of Glen's problems was immediately recognizable. You could count on him to jump up as soon as his name was called with one question on his mind: "When do we eat?" he asked with a grin. That was his usual opening line. He was some forty pounds overweight and always fighting a losing battle with the school and his mom over his diet.

I could savor this moment, as I gave Glen some kind of reply, while looking around at my male volunteers. I knew every one of them was saying a prayer that they would not be in his cabin this year. One of my volunteers was not bothering to pray because he knew he didn't have "a prayer!" Doug Cantu had worked with Glen last year, and Doug knew I liked to keep campers and counselors together if possible. It was possible.

Because of his easy-going nature and good sense of humor, we all liked to be around Glen during his waking hours. The reason nobody wanted to be in his cabin was because they knew a good night's sleep was most likely out of the question. Glen was occasionally referred to as "Freight Train." He did not get this nickname because of the size of his nose; rather, he had the legendary ability to keep an entire cabin awake with his snoring.

Well, actually, Glen did give his cabin-mates a sporting chance. Over the last two years, we had made kind of a game about it. The key was to go to sleep before Glen. If you were able to do so, there was a good chance you might get a few hours in dreamland. However, if Glen got to sleep first, you could just about hang it up. That is, until the early morning hours when you would finally drop off into a slumber born of exhaustion. That usually occurred about twenty minutes before the morning alarm clock would go off. Glen's bunkmates did their best to keep him lying on his side. It was on his back that he really began to rumble like a slow-moving freight train. Over and over again, poor Glen got called back from his solid sleep by someone telling him to turn on his side and shut up!

I once heard Steve Skinner tell a friend who had asked if he ever had to spend the night in Glen's cabin, "Yes, I once spent a night in Glen's cabin.

It was the worst two weeks of my life!"

The really frustrating part of this whole shebang was the realization that even if you did beat Glen to sleep, there was no guarantee you would stay in such a blissful state throughout the night. Odds were that he would have to go to the bathroom at least once.

Above: "Glen Braxton, 14...receives swimming instruction from his counselor Celeste Huffines," reads the *Daily Press* caption.

Below: Deanna and Charles Turner, also in the *Daily Press*

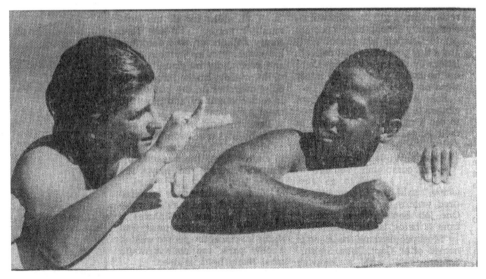

Campers With A Special Cause

'What They Wanted Was ... To Be Like Everyone Else'

By Betsy Raper
Staff Writer

A lazy sun rose slowly over the quiet, woodsy campground. The trees yawned and stretched in the slight breeze.

Birds chirped overhead and down by the river the water lapped gently at the banks.

By 9:30 on this Sunday morning the piece of rolling meadowland in Middlesex County, known as Camp Piankatank, was wide awake, ready for an onslaught of campers.

The camp is owned by the Virginia Baptist General Association and is normally used by church youth groups, but today's campers were 30 blind or deaf children and 55 counselors and leaders.

The day, organized by Mike Haywood, director of Youth and Family Servies for the Peninsula Baptist Association, was designed to let the children experience canoeing, swimming, scuba diving and archery, to give them a chance to be with friends and enjoy a stroll down a quiet wooded path.

It didn't take long for the campers to spread to all parts of the campground. Always nearby each of the children was a counselor — ready to lend a hand, to offer encouragement.

"But," counselor Maryanne Williams said, "the last thing they (the handicapped) wanted from us was pity. What they wanted was to have fun, to be like everybody else."

For those who couldn't see, the archery range was an added challenge. Occasionally an arrow would hit the target and cheers from the onlookers encouraged the archers.

The trip to the swimming pool was the noisiest and most enjoyed of the day's activities.

Haywood and his group of youth volunteers from local Baptist churches and Campus Life have provided other activities for area deaf and blind children during the past two years. There was a weekend camp this summer, ski trips during the winter and some of the deaf youngsters are members of a softball team that Haywood coaches.

Many of the children come from the Virginia School at Hampton, while others have journeyed to camp outs from as far away as Richmond.

Two of the older deaf girls have joined Mike's group of counselors to help with blind children.

Counselors' responsibilities include being the eyes or ears for their charge. It means being there to take a child who cannot see into the swimming pool; to touch a deaf child's shoulder as a signal for lunch.

It means encouraging a newcomer to take a chance.☐

8
The Bathroom

I am being a little unfair to Glen on the bathroom part. It could just as easily be any of the other campers who would need to make the potty run. This was a possibility all of the campers lived with. Sometimes we needed go only as far as the edge of the porch; but there were other times when we had to take the long hike to the bathroom on the hill. And, as mentioned, the longest hike was the one from Asia.

(Some years ago, they built several new cabins and even a new dining hall. The nicest feature of the new cabins was indoor plumbing. Still, I have always felt that my newer volunteers missed out on a unique experience. They do not agree!)

Many a time, one of us would find ourselves walking down the path half asleep, with a camper holding onto the back of our elbow. On the way to our destination, we would encounter another pair, in the same configuration, returning to their cabin. Too sleepy to speak, we acknowledged each other with a slight nod.

I do remember a few things...the long walks to get to our cabins. One night on our way to the cabin, a camper and I were separated from our group who had the flashlights. So my "blind" camper led us back to the cabin! (A humbling experience!) Of course, there was the time another camper tried to lead us back, and I let her walk into a tree (by accident)! There was the night we had "the screamer" in our cabin. I don't think this poor girl had ever been in "the wilderness" before. Every time a bug flew near her, she would jump off the top bunk, screaming and flopping her hands. It made me realize how truly "brave" these kids were allowing teenagers to lead them into the wild where nothing was familiar.

—Jeri

A little side note to the bathroom scenes: In the mid-nineties, we were still holding the retreats. One year, a fellow by the name of John came with the Richmond group and asked if I remembered him. I did, and as it turned out, he had attended several times during the early eighties. During one of our conversations, John told me how he was always able to remember the name of Camp Piankatank—"When you go to the bathroom for a *pee*, don't forget to *yank* on a *tank*." John is a Craig Waddell kind of guy!

Of course, if you were not the one with Glen holding onto your arm, you would feel secure in the knowledge that you could return to your cabin and drop back off to sleep again. So I guess Doug had a right to give me a dirty look when I called out his name. Next, I put two more vision-impaired guys in the cabin with Glen. They would be paired with female volunteers during the day.

I put Max with Andrea Enzor. Max had been with Andrea the last year, and he had developed a crush on her. Because of the number of girls who volunteered, we often had females working with guys during the day. It always seemed to work out fine, and the vision-impaired guys didn't seem to mind a bit. Putting the two of them together again would make Max's weekend. He was fortunate, as there was not a more caring person than Andrea.

Susan Ball and
Becky Hogge

9
Learning to Sign

ext, I put Lloyd, who would also bunk in Asia, with two girls. Lloyd was a special fellow. He was both hearing and visually impaired, and only the second such person we had worked with on the retreats.

The first was a girl, whose name I have unfortunately forgotten. What I have not forgotten about her is that she was the young lady who got us interested in the hearing impaired. She had come with the group from Richmond the second year we held our retreat. She had been born hearing impaired and was beginning to go blind. She was suffering from a disease that is referred to as "tunnel vision." She could see only straight ahead with very little peripheral vision. What peripheral vision she did have would continue to decrease with time. The size of her tunnel would grow smaller and smaller.

She still had a good degree of vision when she came on that retreat. This young lady gave the rest of us our first introduction to sign language in a most unusual way. None of us knew a bit of sign language, except for Josie O'Kane, who was beginning to learn through her college courses in speech pathology. Naturally, Josie got go look after her for the weekend.

It turned out that our new camper had quite a temper. Every time she did not like something or someone, she had a quick three-word sentence for the occasion. Since she could not speak, it was her fingers and hands that let you know of her displeasure. In rapid-fire succession, she would place the first two fingers of her right hand on top of the same two left hand fingers; then all four fingers of the right hand on the back of her left hand; and finally, the tip of her right little finger on the center of her left palm. She did it so quick that it took us all day to pick up the signs, but soon we all knew how to sign, "Sit on it!"

Josie took it all good-naturedly, but she made sure we all knew what her camper was going through.

I sure wish I could relate some of the very inspiring phrases, learned in sign, which led us in this direction. The truth is that we all got caught up in signing this new insult—"Sit on it." This was great because you could impart your displeasure from far away.

The retreat was held the first part of June. For the rest of the summer, it was a common occurrence to pull up next to a friend at a stoplight and exchange "Sit-on-its!" Still, it had a beneficial side effect, because by the end of the summer, a bunch of us decided we wanted to learn more signs. (Even some that were not insults!)

We got Josie to teach us what she had learned. That September, Josie began her field placement at the Virginia School for the Deaf and Blind. She got to know several parents of hearing-impaired children, and they began to bring their children to her parents' house for our sign-language sessions.

Suddenly, we had found a whole new group of friends. There was one of Josie's students we did not meet—Shannon. Josie had told us about her, and she had tried, without success, to get the girl's address from the school. Shannon was now in public school, but Josie did not know where. She told us we had really missed out by not getting to meet her.

We didn't miss out on some other really neat people, however—kids like Marcia Ashley and Ronnie Tucker and Tina Steele. We took them and some others with us on our next retreat.

Top left: Josie and her camper, who got us interested in signing

Top right: Josie and Susan—hugging was the ongoing camp activity.

Above: Three campers who were also best friends—Shannon, Marcia, and Tina

Opposite: Vicki Tomlin

Above: Sandy Squibb (Bob Moore to the right without a shirt)

Below: James and Denise Harris

10

Lloyd

*I*t took a lot of patience to work with Lloyd, but I had just the two for the job. One was a young lady with long black hair and a radiant smile. Most of the guys at some point had been in love with Elise Alfaro. She handled it well and flirted with everyone. She was able to do that with such finesse that she kept herself out of hot water. But she did most of her flirting with John Hogge. They eventually got married and now have daughters. Elise, who would eventually graduate from nursing school, was a very resourceful and caring person.

I first met Elise at her high school when I was working as a Campus Life volunteer. Campus Life is a non-denominational Christian organization, which works with high-school students. Ralph Talton and I had gone by the school on a Thursday morning at lunch period to talk with some of the students. We were planning a hike that weekend and needed to find out just who would be going.

Standing outside the cafeteria, talking with a dozen or so students, I noticed this long-haired girl standing just outside the crowd, listening to us. The rest of the group were regular club attendees, but I had not seen her before. She looked like she was interested, and so I asked her if she would like to go on the hike with us. She said yes and seemed excited.

I then went through my usual routine of questions for such occasions. I asked her if she would like to come to the club meeting that night, did she need a ride, would she like to play softball, and would she be interested in helping with some of our ministries to the handicapped. She beamed and answered, "E. All of the above."

It was obvious to me that she would fit right in with the rest. Of course, that didn't mean I would have no trouble with her name. That night, I gave her a ride home from club and kept talking about everything we were involved with. She didn't say much. (OK, so she didn't have time to get in a reply, and she was too new to realize she would have to just butt right in!) However, as she got out of the car, she told me, "Everything sounds wonderful, Mike. But please stop calling me Alise. My name is Elise!"

Above: Craig and I help Danae Waters across.

Left: From *Crusader Magazine* (Jan. '94), artist rendition of Bill Sinclair, Wes Garrett, Kathy Smith, Nathan, myself, and Chuck Paul

11
Making New Friends

This is probably as good a time as any to talk a little about "The Group." During this time, there were about thirty or forty of us that hung together a lot. Of that number, at any given time, twenty-five or so did almost *everything* together. We never had an official name or status for our assembled members, but most referred to us as "The Group."

The Group consisted mostly of high school and college students, with a few adults thrown into the mix. (Some people would question the word *adult* when referring to members of the Group, including yours truly!) I must confess that the majority were girls, most of whom played for me in a city softball league. This did help attract several guys to the Group, who were top-notch fellows.

A lot of the Group were members of our Baptist churches, although many were from other denominations. Others I had met through Campus Life and were not yet members of a church. They soon would be. We had a smattering of Catholics, Methodists, Church of Christ members, and other denominations, as well as some from non-denominational churches. All in all, it was pretty much an ecumenical group hanging around a Southern Baptist. They made up the core of volunteers for my ministries to the handicapped. Those ministries included several weekly events, as well as the summer retreats and field trips.

The majority, though not all, were also part of Campus Life. On Friday and Saturday nights, my apartment became a hangout for whoever did not have a date. Needless to say, I wasn't dating at all at the time, or most anytime for that matter. We would go out to a movie or to play hide-and-seek at the local park. Going out to eat or renting a video were also big events. Games, such as Risk and Clue, as well as multifarious card games, carried on into all hours of the night and morning. The record number gathered in my apartment was forty-four, watching a VCR movie.

For a short period of time, my apartment became a Saturday evening bedroom for a group of guys. That was a time when Pete, Steve, John, Troy, Bill, Scott, and whoever else would spend all day Saturday officiating football or softball. We would get home in the late afternoon, meet for dinner, and then go back to my apartment to watch a movie. We would turn on the flick and lie all over the floor and couches to watch. Twenty minutes later, every one of us would be fast asleep. Unless the phone rang, we would not awaken until static replaced the gentle hum of the movie audio. Then we would get up, and everyone would head for home and bed.

Anyone could be part of the Group, as long as they enjoyed being with us; working with kids and the handicapped; playing softball, if they were girls (regardless of ability—we once had a three-year record of 4–41); and were willing to put up with our offbeat sense of humor. (And Craig Waddell's puns.) A large majority took my YMCA lifeguarding course. This was important, too, as most of our retreats were water-oriented.

A lot of the teens first got involved by asking to help with one of the ministries, and then they usually started hanging out with the Group. A few, like Stel Washburn, showed up at a softball practice and then stayed around forever. Stel came with Ike Newingham, the Campus Life director. Part of her attire on that first Saturday morning practice made me certain that she was meant to be a part of the Group. She was wearing an old pair of jeans with a full-size football patch sewed into the seat. I mean, this was obviously a girl we could kick around. We soon found out that this girl was very good at kicking back!

I also got to know Jimmy George through Ike Newingham (Campus Life/Youth for Christ club leader at Menchville High School. Ike, who was the overall director of Campus Life on the Peninsula, and I were driving a busload of Menchville cheerleaders (honest, this was Ike's idea) to an away football game. The morning of the trip, someone had egged the bus. So, when we got to the school, Ike saw a student and asked him to help me clean the bus, since Ike said he had other things to do. That student was Jimmy George. Later, he came out to a softball practice and never went away. (I think I am glad the bus got egged that morning.)

I got to know Elizabeth Union because she told funny jokes. One day on the Living End (a Campus Life week-long skiing trip between Christmas and New Year's), riding to the ski slopes, I was standing on the bus talking to a blonde young lady who was reading a Stephen King novel that I had read earlier in the year. She told me I could sit on her lap. That is how I met Danae Waters.

I met Pete Smith because of a snowstorm. I guess I actually met him because Ike brought Pete's older sister Kathy out to play on the ball team. She became part of the Group. The snowstorm canceled school for the day. Several of the students from Campus Life got together and asked me for a ride. I don't remember where we went, but Kathy asked if her seventh-grade brother could tag along. He showed up, a shaggy blond kid, and we could never get rid of him.

Guys like Pete and Jimmy George hung around because they knew a lot of good-looking girls were always present. A few I met because it just seemed like the Lord was telling me to do so. That was true of the Sisters Paschal. I first met them in a high-school parking lot.

At the time, a dozen of us were swimming with mentally challenged kids at the YMCA. I would pick up most of the gang at school each Thursday afternoon. For a couple of weeks, while waiting for the last of my helpers to exit the school, Karen and Shannon Paschal would walk past the van. They would always say hi to me and those in the van as they headed for their car. One day, as we were leaving the parking lot, it hit me that I should ask them if they wanted to help us at the pool. The next week I did—and they did! Then I asked them to play ball and take lifeguarding and come to Campus Life...well, I did not have to ask them about the latter. They had been coming to club meetings for several weeks. I had just not met them yet.

Several people got involved in the Group because of the handicapped swim class. Deanna D'Urso knew a few of the early helpers, and she asked to join in. I was all for that.

Elise Alfaro and Andrea Enzor were hanging around and playing softball for me. They brought a friend with them to practice one evening. Their friend had her glove with her and asked if she could shag a few flies. I said, "Why not." A half hour later, John Whitsel came up and said only one person had caught any flies so far, and that was Andrea's friend. I said, "Hey, would you like to…?" And that's how I met Kelly Williams. I could go on, but we have to draw the line somewhere, at least as far as this chapter goes.

Above: Jill Godfrey, Heather Ewing, and Karen Watts
Below: Caroline Lawson and a camper play the game "Darling, If You Loved Me."

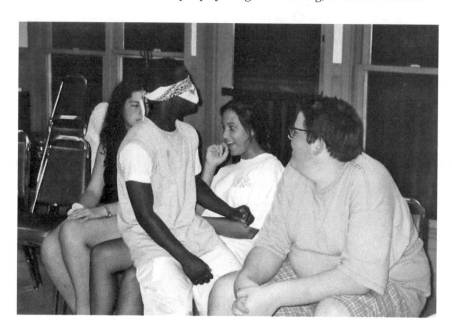

12
Shannon

I put Elise with Lloyd because she has an abundance of patience, as did her co-counselor, Shannon Riddle. Shannon, herself hearing impaired, was an athletic girl who absolutely did not allow hearing loss to keep her from doing anything. It was through Steve Skinner that I first met Shannon.

Steve called me one Thursday night before a weekend retreat we had planned. He said he had done something and hoped it would be all right with me. I immediately wondered what kind of sneaky thing he was up to that would prompt this kind of call. Steve proceeded to tell me that he had met two deaf teenagers at his pool the week before, and they had later dropped by his house to visit. Both lived near his home. Steve promptly invited Shannon and her friend Ronnie Tucker to come on the retreat. They immediately said yes. So, Steve wasn't calling to get an OK from me; he was just letting me know to prepare for two more spaces. He had already invited them. That was fine with me. (Most of my helpers were free spirits!)

The next day, I told Josie about Steve's phone call and she exclaimed, "Mike! That's the girl I have been telling you about. You will love her." Shannon was the girl from school that Josie had been trying to find. She hadn't met Ronnie yet but said he would undoubtedly be super. And he was. Both Shannon and Ronnie became involved in a lot of our activities, including the retreats and Campus Life.

That weekend was their first event with us. Before the retreat was over, both had made lasting friendships within the Group. Ronnie was working after school and could not get quite as involved, but he was always around. Shannon, who was not working, got involved in everything—*everything!*

The first afternoon of the retreat, Josie and I were playing kickball with some of the smaller kids. John Whitsel and the rest of the studs were playing softball with the older ones. For the second time, John came up to me and said I had better come watch someone play softball. He went on to say that Shannon could hit the ball harder than anyone on our team, with the exception of Kelly Williams. So, I turned to Josie and learned how to sign a few key sentences. You know, the ones that start with "Would you like to…?" Shannon nodded her head and bobbed her fist, meaning "Yes!"

Shannon, Elise, and Lloyd would make a great team. I just had to be sure I had someone in the boys' cabin to look out for Lloyd at night. I continued on with the rest of the assignments for Asia. I had already decided that, since they couldn't hear him snore, I would put five of the younger hearing-impaired kids in with Glen. They didn't mind at all. Of course, their counselors were less than thrilled. Doug Cantu, Pete Smith, Steve Burnette, and Jimmy George would have to look after the five of them, as well as Lloyd and their own campers.

Several of the girl counselors had already claimed dibs on the deaf boys. That left me two more spaces for volunteers. When I had filled out all the bunk space for Asia, there was a collective sigh of relief from the rest of the males present.

I didn't realize it at the time I snapped this photo, but one of my counselors is telling the other she just got propositioned by a vision-impaired camper.

13
Disco 85 & Zippy

*T*he next cabin was Paraguay. This was the nickname cabin.

"Piano Man," I said, "you are with Scott Millar. Swamp Dog and Steve Hayes. Disco 85 and Donald Hux. Bird Dog and Bill Bowman. And last but not least, Big Al and Craig Waddell. You guys try to keep it down tonight. The rest of us want to get some sleep."

Big Al might be totally blind, but I could have sworn I saw a mischievous gleam in his eye. I dismissed it as imagination. I should have paid more attention.

This gang was some of the students that Dean, Larry, and Craig had driven out of the school parking lot that afternoon. Not only did they have some cool nicknames, but several of them were among the better wrestlers in the state, sighted or blind! As with most of the visually impaired, they were gifted musicians, who never failed to entertain us at the talent show. And, oh yes, they did have something special planned for the campfire that first night, as we shall see. Fortunately, I had a number of guys who could hold their own physically with most anyone, and that always came in handy.

∽

Now, don't think that the nicknames were meant only for those we helped. Many of my own counselors were also given names, and often by us, their so-called friends. One of these was the name we gave to a really cute and helpful young lady named Tracy Freeland. One of the more dependable volunteers, she got her nickname during our swimming ministry to the mentally challenged at the YMCA.

One of the boys, Tony, had been to the bathroom and just returned to the lobby. We were trying to gather all the kids into the locker room. It was like trying to make an ocean wave move away from the shore. While all this was going on, Tony had been alternating between looking down at his shoes and up at the lobby. As things began to clear out, he took a little more interest in his surroundings. Then he began to inch toward Tracy Freeland until, finally, he was standing in front of her. He continued to look down. I had no idea what his problem was. Tracy, on the other hand, was observant enough to see the object of his attention. That turned out to be her undoing. Tony's fly was unzipped, and he needed help zipping it up.

At this point, Tracy made a major mistake—a mistake that would haunt her for years. She did the right thing and zipped him up. But from that day on, whenever Tony's fly was down, he made a beeline for Miss Tracy, and then stand silently in front of her until she helped him out.

(Within a year, we had gone to a two-day-per-week ministry with this group. It never took us long to get totally involved in anything. Thursdays were always swimming. On Tuesdays, we would rotate between such activities as roller skating, bowling, horseback riding, putt-putt, and fishing. This meant that Tony and his zipper were around quite a bit.)

It would not have been all that bad if we had left it alone. Of course, we didn't. When did we ever give anyone a break? We kept kidding Tracy about her zipper friend, and then we gave her a nickname: Zippy! And to Tracy's everlasting chagrin, we even used it in her sign language name, which was a signed T moving upward in a zipping motion. I felt it was a real help to her to have a "sign name" she could share with the hearing-impaired kids on our retreats. Tracy never saw it as an advantage.

Above left: Tammy Martin, who later married Jim George, poses at the pool. This photo proves that Jim married up! *Above right:* Smith lifeguards with high-fashion sunglasses.

Below: Susan Dolan plays in the pool with a camper.

Top: Bob Jensen
and James

Left: Bob Jensen
in a photo by Ev-
erett Hullum for
MissionsUSA (an
SBC publication),
December 1979

14
Swimming

*I*t took about fifteen minutes to give out all the cabin assignments and get people moving toward their quarters, where they could pick out their bunks. Then, they knew to change into bathing suits and head for the first activity of the retreat: the Friday afternoon swim. The swimming pool was always one of the major attractions at this retreat.

On two occasions, the Friday afternoon swim started the retreat off with a real bang. The first was the time that I told Pete Smith to lifeguard while I was getting everything sorted out. Pete decided he to take it easy and not change into swimming trunks. He figured nothing bad ever happened on the first night.

Doug Cantu also showed up, not suited out. However, his camper Nathan (this was before Doug had the pleasure of working with Glen) was ready to hit the water. Doug told Pete that he was not going to swim until after we ate but that he would watch Nathan. Nathan asked if he could jump off the diving board. Pete couldn't remember if Nathan could swim or not, and so he asked. Nathan said that he could and that he had gone off the diving board before. Pete told him to go ahead.

Nathan, led by Doug, climbed up on the board and slowly walked to the end, where he put his toes over the edge. Pete cautioned him to jump straight out, and Nathan nodded. He did jump straight out. And he hit the water. And he sunk to the bottom of the pool. And he stayed there.

Pete and Doug walked to the edge and looked down, waiting for him to push off the bottom. He didn't seem to be panicking, but neither did he seem in a hurry to head back to the surface. At that point, Pete and Doug entered into a conversation about who was responsible to jump in with their clothes on, if such a move was necessary. Pete said it was Doug's duty as Nathan's counselor. Doug replied that Pete was the lifeguard, and that meant he had to. Doug's point won out. (This back-and-forth actually only took a couple seconds.)

Pete finally decided that Nathan was in a bit of trouble (indeed he was) and dove down to rescuc him. Nathan remained calm as he was helped out and said he thought he had known how to swim, but he had been wrong. Still he wasn't worried, since he knew one of the guys would come get him. Pete closed the pool until after dinner.

~

Jimmy George had a more exciting time when he and Marianne Williams went alone for a quick pre-camper dip on a Friday night. Marianne was quite happy no one else was around because, when she jumped off the diving board and hit the water, the bottom of her two-piece came off. Despite her cries of distress, Jimmy made her dive down to the bottom of the deep end to get it. Thankfully, she was fully presentable by the time the kids arrived.

~

We had so many attendees this year, I had to put four of the girl counselors in the infirmary. That left one of the large tents for Jim Ailor, Bill Sinclair, Chuck Paul, Larry van Wyngarden, Dean Jernigan, and myself. The tents were spacious and made a nice place to spend the night—hopefully without disturbance. We changed and headed for the swimming pool, where things went remarkably smooth. That should have alerted me for later on.

The pool was probably the most popular site at camp, both for campers and counselors. One of the highlights of each retreat was when we brought scuba gear in and let everyone try it. (Many of my Florida Keys buddies first tried scuba at Camp Piankatank.)

Years of muddy creek diving had taught us that you did not have to be able to see underwater in order to enjoy the experience and do so safely. Also, a few years earlier, I had read an article about a Swedish hard-hat diver, who taught blind adults to use diving gear in order to do work in a harbor where visibility was nonexistent. He found that they could work with no problems or hang-ups. We found that our own group took to it fantastically. Their response was so enthusiastic that we often emptied three or four tanks in a hour during our first swim time.

We worked carefully and diligently to teach the correct use of the gear. They were apt pupils. Naturally, we began in shallow water; but in a short time, we would have them swimming at the bottom of the deep end with calm assurance. They didn't want to come to the surface and would have stayed under until the air ran out. Usually, we had to call time so that others could try it. (The first time I had done this was not at the pool. I had gotten Jay Lawson—of the hoped-for Jay Lawson/Jimmy Ailor co-pastor team—to lug my tank down the steep path at Eastover to the James River, where we used the equipment on our first day out with the blind.

You asked about our memories, and I've been thinking hard…. I remember so few real moments in time, but the general impression of some of the best times of my life. The experience of being with youth from other churches, the music we had (especially the blind musicians), campfires, s'mores, archery, crabbing, fishing, canoeing, and a chance to try scuba diving! …I was always amazed at how well the blind/deaf students joined into activities. Several excelled at scuba diving, an experience I felt was claustrophobia….

—Jeri

One of the other great things about the pool was some of the bathing suits on display. Kelly Johnson's red one-piece was the most popular by far, though Elise's was not far behind. I think Angela DeLara had the bathing suit we all wished had been worn at the pool. Alas, she only used that for sunbathing at home! Another story for another time.

Top: Doug Cantu runs with a camper during a softball game. *Above:* Cayla Campbell gives a little extra TLC. *Left:* Steve Hayes waits below.

54

15
Doug Panics

*O*ur pool time had begun with a June sun still shining above the tree line; but within an hour, dark, ugly clouds had overtaken the sun and advanced toward the camp. We continued with the scuba and general pool fun while keeping an eye on the gathering storm. I was hoping it would just blow over. Then, out behind the archery range, the first bolt of lightning flashed out of an ominous black cloud.

Hey, I know the answer to that one! I sent everyone scattering for their cabins. Even Howard and Edrick jumped out of the pool when told (signed) to. They had seen the lightning, too. I was glad they wanted no part of it while in the pool.

I was pleased to see that we had completely vacated the pool area by the time the clouds came to a halt over the center of camp. Whatever else they might have in store for me this weekend, I could rely on this group of volunteers to move swiftly and efficiently whenever it really counted. It looked like it might not rain, though we were now being treated to a beautiful light show in the skies overhead. Most of the lightning was within the cloud banks, giving a strobe effect. I yelled for the counselors to get everybody changed and meet back at the dining hall.

John Whitsel and John Hogge crossed my path, pushing a wheel-chair-bound kid. They were the last ones to get out of the pool gate, but they had the shortest distance to get to their cabin. This was one of the few situations when having a greater number of girl counselors caused a bit of confusion. However, even as the wind picked up again in a swirling pattern, those girls with boy campers guided their kids to the appropriate cabin. There, they turned them over to their male counterparts.

The one exception to this scene was four girls in pursuit of two little boys. The boys seemed to be blown by the wind, running across the center of the field with their arms up, invoking the skies to open up. Right behind them came the two Kellys—Johnson and Williams—along with Deanna D'Urso and Susan Dolan.

The rain dancers were Donald and Jeff. They were two of the hearing-impaired kids we had picked up at the McDonald's on the way to camp. These two, along with Edrick and Howard and a boy named Waylon, made up a five-some who could keep you going the entire weekend. Waylon had a pot belly, which seemed to bounce up and down in rhythm with his walk. His physique had earned him the nickname "The Whale." By the end of the weekend, the counselors who had been with these five were usually in a state of exhaustion—happy exhaustion, but exhaustion nonetheless.

Hey, time does march on. About ten years later, Waylon graduated from high school. He was in the area and wanted something to do. I was running a sports camp and got Waylon to help Chris Ellis, a newer Smishy, teach flag football at the camp. (I should probably mention that *Smishy* is a contraction for "Summer Missionary." Each summer, I had a team of four to six college students who worked for the Peninsula Baptist Association as summer missionaries. A couple dozen people mentioned in this account spent one to four years as a Smishy. The name was coined by the grandmother of one of my Smishies in the 1970s.)

Knowing that Jeff and Donald would soon be corralled and seeing that everyone else seemed to be making their way to their own cabins, I thought it best to head for my own tent. One drawback to the tents were that they had no electricity. However, when I arrived, I found Chuck Paul lighting a Coleman lantern.

The next bolt of lightning turned the disadvantage to an advantage. I watched a shaft of electricity dive down at a spot near us, followed by an immediate burst of thunder. Then, a split second later, a blanket of darkness fell over the camp.

Doug Cantu was in the middle of his cabin when the lights went out. As I have mentioned, Asia is located a bit far back in the woods, where tall trees crowd in close to the walls. With the dark clouds already robbing the cabin of what little late-afternoon light it would normally have, he was engulfed in almost total darkness. The cabin became silent, and you could hear the wind whipping through the trees, sounding somewhat like a locomotive roaring by.

Inside, all were motionless. It was Doug who finally broke the silence. (He later related this to me.) Doug was now immersed in the sightless world of his cabin-mates, and he didn't like it one bit. Doug's flashlight was out on the front porch, doing him no good at all. The surprise of being caught in the dark caused him to lose all sense of direction.

In a brief moment of panic, Doug shouted, "Oh, my God! Oh no! Oh, my God! The lights have all gone out! What am I going to do?" (This was one of Doug's favorite expressions when in a panicked situation. Several years later, some of us were treading water during a dive at the Keys. Suddenly, Doug's face showed an expression of panic. He repeated, almost verbatim, the same phrase, while adding the fact that a big barracuda was swimming through my legs. Much to my relief, it turned out to be a harmless baby!)

Glen, who had been holding onto Doug's elbow during this shouting, now placed his other hand on Doug's shoulder.

"That's OK," he said, "we know what to do. Our lights went out a long time ago!"

The laughter that echoed through the cabin dissipated the tension.

"Right," replied Doug with a smile no one could see.

"If I could find my flashlight, I could get us squared away," said Jimmy George.

Doug replied, "If I could find the door, I could get a flashlight. Mine's on the front porch. I am going to feel my way to it."

"Hey, guys. We can help you out. The door is off to my left," said Max, who had been silent to this point.

Meanwhile, in one of the lower bunks in the far corner, Steve Burnette was too preoccupied with Lloyd to even worry about Doug's dilemma. Being deaf and blind, you had to sign or spell words into his hands. Steve's signing ability wasn't the greatest, and he was slowly explaining the situation to Lloyd. I could tell you several stories about Steve in the dark, but I won't. Suffice it to say, it was a good thing that Steve had something to take his mind off the darkness.

Well, fine, just one story. Many years later, I took a group of guys with me to Key Largo to go snorkeling. One night, we told ghost stories. Steve was in the midst of telling us that he was not scared in the least. Just then, the lights went out, and of course, there was the weird noise of the air conditioner winding down, which did sound spooky. The lights came back on, and there was Steve sitting in Pete Smith's lap!

Glen said, "Max is right. Tell them, Max."

"OK," he said, his voice taking on the tone of a patient teacher. As would often happen on these outings, the role of camper and helper had, for the moment, been reversed. "What everybody needs to do is stop and relax for a second."

Pete and Jimmy said in unison, "We are relaxed!" I suppose they were as relaxed as anyone could be, sitting on a bunk with five deaf kids crawling all over them.

Max continued, "I never heard you close the door, so I'm assuming that it's open."

"It is," Doug said.

"Good. Now, what you need to do next is turn around until you face the door. Remember, you will be using your sense of feel, and you should be able to notice a slight draft on your face. The way the wind is blowing, you can probably feel it on any part of your body. Of course, there might even be a shade of lightness at the door. I can't use that cue at all, though—only what I can feel."

The next few seconds were silent except for the sound of several pairs of shoes shuffling around in the dark. "It works!" was the sudden exclamation from Doug's general area. "Max, you are a genius!"

"We learn all sorts of things like that at the rehab center," added Glen.

Doug was in the middle of telling everyone to hang on for a second while he made his way to the door, when it all became academic. The lights came back on. Everyone cheered or signed happily. Jimmy and Pete disengaged themselves from the ten pairs of arms and legs, and the group went about the task of getting changed into dry clothing.

After knocking out the lights for a few minutes, the storm moved on, and by the time we had gathered for dinner, the sky was clear again. It had not rained more than a few drops, which meant we could carry on with all of our evening programming, including the outdoor campfire.

Above: Diane Sexton
Below: Denise Harris, Holly Thompson, Dreamer Johnson, and Susan Wallace are backup singers for James.

Above: Wesley leads Stuart Bradley, Bret Godfrey, and the guy campers.

Below: Alan Butts practices with campers for the talent show.

16
The Talent Show

*A*fter dinner, a period of activities led into a time of preparation for the annual talent show. We always held that in the dining hall. Usually, after the sun had gone down, it was cool enough to be comfortable. The piano wasn't tuned, the acoustics were awful, and you had to speak over the drone of a gigantic wall fan. However, I think most of us remember the talent show as a good time.

Over the years, we were treated to some mighty fine talent…and some not so mighty fine talent. Both the good and the bad were generally emceed by Bill Sinclair, sometimes referred to as "Harmonica Man." After Bill left for Nashville, this duty was taken over by Doug Cantu and his sax. Forms of entertainment have included singing, music, skits, jokes, and overall off-the-wall events.

The talent shows are one of those events for which I cannot recall a lot of the particulars (as Jeri Hudson said in her letter). Rather, I recall the feeling of unity, joy, and appreciation for good friends and the love of Jesus. We could always count on Sinclair to play some superb harmonica, along with his saxophone and guitar. Then he would get to tricks and play two harmonicas at once, one completely inside his mouth and one at his nose. Others, like Doug Cantu, would come along later and bring their own musical instrument for our pleasure.

Still, I think what we remember the most was the fantastic music, both sung and played, by the visually impaired. We could also count on the hearing impaired to come up with several good skits.

One great moment in the annual talent show included the time we performed a skit involving three different emotions in three different segments using the same dialogue. During a break, we looked back toward the stage area and saw four of our hearing-impaired kids re-enacting the skit. They hadn't gotten all the words down, but they copied the actions and emotions perfectly. We stood there in awe and watched them do a better job than the volunteers who had first performed it. I can also vividly remember David Cromer and Eric Wilson performing the "There Is a Man Without" skit, as well as the night that Burnette, Smith, Millar, and I surprised Cherie Bradley by singing at her feet.

There were three songs that became synonymous with camp. Two were written and sung by Sinclair. One was called the "Rebate Song," a clever play on the then new practice of automobile dealers giving rebates. (Yes, this was a while ago.) Some of the best lines go something like this: "Don't brag about the money you saved when you brought your brand-new Ford. / Let me tell you 'bout the life I saved when I turned on to the Lord." The second song is a beautiful Christian ballad, titled "More Than a Lifetime."

Both of these songs are inspirational, but the one probably most identified with camp is a little less so. It was Chuck Paul who first told us about the song "Rum by Gum." We always began each talent show by singing this wonderfully edifying song!

We're coming, we're coming, our own little band.
On the right side of temperance, we do take our stand.
We don't chew tobacco because we do think
That the people who use it are likely to drink.

(Chorus) Away, away with rum, by gum, with rum, by gum, with rum, by gum.
Away, away with rum, by gum. The song of the Temperance Union!

We never eat cookies because they have yeast,
And one little bite turns a man to a beast.
We cannot imagine a graver disgrace
Than a man in the gutter with crumbs on his face.
(Chorus)

We never eat fruit cake because it has rum,

And one little bite turns a man to a bum.
We cannot imagine a sorrier sight,
Than a man eating fruit cake until he gets tight.
(Chorus)

Dear Mike,

True story. I heard on the radio Tuesday, "Away with Rum by Gum." Can you believe it?

Marianne Williams (from Texas)

Sandy Squibb, Lynn Scott, Joyce Mayes, and Celeste Huffines sing while Tracy Ferguson plays for the talent show.

Top: Jeremy tries out Bill's harmonica.

Left: Elise, Craig, and Jim George help Mr. Flood on a hike.

17
The Campfire

After the talent show, we headed out to the campfire area. This night's program would feature more singing and ghost stories. The next would be the night for s'mores and a campfire worship service, led by Jimmy Ailor.

I have always regarded the campfires as one of the more relaxing periods on our retreats. It was a special time for friends to gather together. The limited light provided by the flickering fire turned all but the closest campers into dim silhouettes.

I told the traditional ghost stories. The camp is located on the edge of what was referred to as the "Haunted Woods." There are supposed to be four buried treasures in the area, each guarded by some sort of ghostly apparition. My stories, a highlight of the first night's campfire activities, would usually go over well. The other major first-night activity was campfire singing, led by Harmonica Man (Bill Sinclair).

I said that *usually* the stories were interesting and well received, even with the hearing-impaired kids. This was not always the case, however. A year later, I would be given a graphic demonstration of that fact. We were in the middle of the ghost-story hour. Howard and Edrick were sitting in the front row. Deanna D'Urso and Annette Alie were signing the stories to them.

Suddenly, Howard got a very serious and worried look on his face. I noticed the look and hoped that the story wasn't too scary for him. After a few minutes of fidgeting, he got up and walked toward me. I didn't know if he was going to stop me or what. But Howard ignored me and walked two or three steps past. Then, in the light of the fire, he proceeded to turn his back on us and take a leak. I tell you what, I can't think of many things that take the mood out of a spooky storytelling session than watching someone take a leak right in front of you.

Howard finished and returned to his seat, still ignoring me. Ten minutes later, Edrick put an end to the stories when he walked up, grabbed my arm, and checked my wristwatch for the time. I decided then that perhaps it was time to head for bed.

Anyway, the stories went well this year, and we moved on from ghosts to songs. Sinclair jumped up in front of the fire and began by giving us a harmonica rendition of a freight train roaring past the campfire. I am sure the staff in Glen Braxton's cabin were thinking that they might get to hear this sound all night long! From there, we moved into a loud songfest. It was a calm and laid-back night, with people spread out all over the area. Still, everyone seemed to be into the singing.

Big Al and his friends had gathered at the back edges, away from the crowd, without any of the counselors to bug them. That was cool. It gave them a chance to be on their own for a little while. From the way they laughed between songs, I figured they were telling some inside jokes. Even that was fine.

The rest of the visually impaired were sitting with sighted friends. Most of the hearing-impaired kids had congregated close to the fire so that they could see Marianne Williams and Cayla Campbell, who were sharing the signing this night. This year, during the ghost stories, the students had not taken their eyes off the girls' hands. That was good. Perhaps everyone, including the counselors, would be a little too spooked to sneak out tonight. (OK, perhaps that thought was a bit naïve.) Now, the girls were signing the songs and any general conversation around the campfire.

Cayla and Marianne were two of my out-of-state summer mission workers. Each year, I got one or two who would work along with our local students. Marianne, whose name I constantly mispronounced as "Murry Ann," was from Texas, while Cayla hailed form Alabama. They were both in Virginia for ten weeks, doing a variety of ministries. These two excellent signers went on to teach the hearing impaired in their home states.

A lot of our local volunteers had also become proficient in signing.

Annette Alie eventually went to Gallaudet University in Washington, D.C., and then on to the Virginia School for the Deaf and Blind. Josie was the first of us to become skilled at signing; she taught the hearing impaired in our area. Kelly Johnson graduated from college in California with a degree in deaf education. Shannon Paschal, Tammy Martin, and several others pursued professions that worked with the hearing impaired. In addition, a lot of the volunteers became excellent signers, which made them invaluable to our ministry: Deanna D'Urso, Angela DeLara, Gail O'Neal, Karen Paschal, Karen Watts, Sandy Squibb, and Mo Johnson, among others. Steve Skinner was probably the best among the guys.

The above list is from the first crew of volunteers to work in the camps. Since then, others, like Andrea Enzor and Deborah Eves and Kelly Ham, have gone in that direction. (And yes, I know I have left out a bunch, though you might be mentioned later on and wish you had been left out altogether!)

Each year, I often got a new person interested in signing. Then, for five to six weeks, I would help them get started in learning sign language. Probably the most important thing I did was to keep them in the company of hearing-impaired people. Invariably, within a short time, their ability would far surpass the teacher's. Then, I would be the one asking, "What was he or she signing to me?" (I can sign slowly, but my mind doesn't seem to function well in that capacity—or in any foreign language for that matter.)

Becky Russell became not only an excellent signer, but she discovered another gift—that of signing songs. She was a lovely girl, whose thin body seemed to flow in a fluid motion as she signed a song. Becky taught this art form to many of our younger volunteers.

Later, we met another Kelly, whose fingers and hands made the spoken word accessible to the hearing impaired. Kelly Ham and her friend Audrey Lamb came to us each summer from a church in Maryland. They had found out about the retreats and came down to spend a week or two working with the summer mission teams. Mrs. Ham or Sue Edelin would bring them down and leave them for a week or so. They also helped on our Smithsonian visits and skiing trips. Neither girl could go more than ten seconds without a big smile breaking out on her face.

I want to tell you about one more of our skilled signing volunteers.

Her name was Cherie Bradley Rice. Cherie was a petite, dark-haired young lady, who I first met through my hearing-impaired friend Shannon Riddle. In fact, there were three girls, all good signers, who started coming to Campus Life at the same time. Cherie, Shannon, and Missy (Dianne Pruitt) were sweet and nice to other people, but they always had a running battle among themselves.

Each week at club, I could hardly wait to find out which one was on the outs with the other two. It didn't always go in an even circle, but you could always count on the fact that a different one would be the "unliked" girl the next week. Over the course of a year, it pretty much balanced itself out. Dianne became quite involved for a while and was one of my better volunteers. Then, as life moved on, so did she, and yet Cherie still hears from her occasionally.

Cherie was one of those people who had a heart of gold and would do anything in the world to help a person, friend or stranger. We used to kid her a lot about being "dizzy," and at times she could really act the part. Come to think of it, a lot of my best girl volunteers were a little dizzy. (For what it is worth, Pete Smith, Steve Burnette, and I always felt that most of Cherie's "dizziness" was an act she put on to keep our attention. It worked!) However, Cherie could run circles around me when it came to signing, and many a time, it was me who felt dizzy trying to follow a conversation between Cherie and Shannon. I relied on Cherie to make me look good. She did.

Anyway, back to the fire. I was sitting there, watching everyone drinking soft drinks and wishing we had made a pot of coffee. It is never too late or too warm for a good cup of steaming black coffee. Well, that would just have to wait for morning. Since no coffee would be forthcoming, I sat and listened to the sound of the singing. The volume would rise and fall from around the campfire, depending on the popularity of the song. Bill played a couple of tunes without lyrics, but for the most part, we were all singing along to the music.

There was one group of voices that seemed to grow stronger with each passing song. Obviously, Big Al and Disco 85 and their gang had given up joke-telling in order to focus their attention to some serious singing. That made sense. They had a good blend of voices, and they did love to sing, as well as listen to a boom box. OK, they were a little loud this night, but that is one of the joys of a camp. You can get as loud as you want and not disturb the neighbors. Bill launched into another song and the five crooning wrestlers in the back raised it another notch.

By the end of that song, I noticed that some of the younger kids were beginning to get a little sleepy. Their counselors were starting to get up, find their campers, and drift off toward the cabins. That signaled the winding down of the songfest. Bill nodded to me and told us that he would close the evening by repeating "More Than a Lifetime." By the time Bill finished that and had begun to pack up his harmonica, it had grown silent around the dying fire. That is, silent except for that outer fringe group. Their voices still boomed out into the night. They had, for sure, enjoyed this evening, and that was the reason we did all this. Now, they had switched to their own songs. I finally sent Craig over to get them moving toward their cabin.

My final task of the night was to grab Chuck and head for a large container of water we used to douse the fire. I was looking for him when I heard Craig cry out. In the darkness, he had tripped over a large object. It turned out to be Big Al, who appeared to have fallen fast asleep right there on the ground. Upon closer observation, however, Big Al wasn't asleep. He was drunk as a skunk and passed out on the ground. He was oblivious to the world, even to the loud refrain of his four buddies, who could still remain upright and sing. Be that as it may, they were not in any condition to walk.

Now we knew why the five had been having such an uproariously good time at the campfire. Someone (that someone turned out to be Big Al himself) had smuggled in a couple of bottles of cheap wine. They had been sipping on it during the campfire. We, in our naïveté, had just assumed this group of guys would be well behaved. This was just another lesson in our education that all people, including the handicapped, are alike in both good and bad ways. (So, let us sing another chorus of "Away with Rum, by Gum!")

This was one of the points I tried to make with my new volunteers—things I learned the hard way. The vision- and hearing-impaired youth, as a whole, were just like the rest of us. They had bad habits, as well as good habits. They might try to sneak in some wine (well, more than just try), do you a good turn, and even lift a few dollars out of your wallet (as did happen on another retreat). They had the same capacity for good and bad behavior, for joys and fears, as well as dreams and goals, as anyone else.

In every respect, they were just like all the other teenagers that hung around me. Although deaf, they enjoyed "talking" on the phone as much as anyone. Except in their case, it was not a phone but a TDD. And that fact leads me to yet another story—a Shannon Riddle story.

Above: Trudy McBride and the guys

Right: Kelly Johnson

18
Shannon's First TDD

If I had any questions about deaf kids "talking" on the phone, it was dispelled by what Shannon's mom told me about her daughter's first TDD. A TDD is a device used with an ordinary phone. Basically, it consists of a keyboard, digital read-out display, and two rubber cups. The receiver is placed so that each end fits into the cups. Both parties have to have a TDD in order to converse. (This was popular in the 1980s but has to some degree been replaced by computers and other electronic devices.)

The very first models stood about four feet high and almost as wide. In fact, the earliest models were little more than reworked army teletype machines (TTY). These first models used printed paper instead of a digital screen. You literally type messages back and forth over the phone lines. Whatever one person types prints on both machines. When you finish a sentence, you type GA, which stands for "Go ahead." That tells the other party that you are ready for them to "speak." When you are ready to end the conversation, you type SK (Stop Keying).

The old machines had one disadvantage for teens. If you forgot to tear off the printed message, your parents could read your entire telephone conversation. (Of course, that wouldn't make any difference in the homes of my volunteers!)

Sometime around 1980, a compact model came out. Teenagers liked this model a lot better because there was no printed record to get you in trouble. It was also more convenient to use and you could take it with you when you went out. Parents liked the new models because they were also cheaper.

To use the portable machine, the person initiating the call places their phone on the TDD and dials the other party's number. A red light on the other machine starts blinking when the phone rings. (Today, a hearing-impaired person can hook their phone up to a lamp. Regardless of whether the lamp is on or off, a ringing phone will make the lamp light flicker. The same can be done with a door bell or to signal an infant crying.)

One of the things we did through the PBA was to purchase about a dozen of these over the years. We were able to let parents see what they were like, lend them to our volunteers who wanted to call their deaf friends, and give them to any hearing impaired who were phone-less.

Shannon's mom told me that when they purchased Shannon's first TDD, they were not sure if she would use it enough to make the purchase worth the money. At the time, they did not use the phone a lot, and so they were in a system in which they got a lower phone rate by being billed per call. As a result, each phone bill had the total number of calls on it. The month after getting the TDD, they had three hundred more calls over their usual amount. Needless to say, they changed to a different phone service.

A lot of the calls were made to a twenty-four-hour hotline crisis center, called Contact Peninsula. Now Shannon's crises, to be sure, were not of an extreme nature. They were merely calls to have a friend come over for the afternoon! Still, this was a crisis of sorts to Shannon, and Contact did have a TDD. In fact, one of Contact's stated services was to act as a relay for persons without TDDs. A hearing-impaired person could call on the TDD and have the Contact worker relay the message on a regular phone, or a hearing person could do the same thing in reverse. (Today, the state has a toll-free number, which specializes as a relay service for the hearing impaired.)

The first time I ever used a TDD was at the Contact Peninsula office. At the time, I was serving as a volunteer counselor for those clients needing face-to-face counseling. I was in the office waiting for a client to show up when one of the workers started using the TDD. She told me it was a girl named Shannon, who was a "regular." I got the worker to give me an on-the-job training course, and I then used my two-finger typing method to talk with Shannon.

I was so thrilled that I asked the PBA for funds to purchase several of the machines. The first year we purchased five, and they were so popular with my volunteers that I could hardly ever keep one for myself; still, I was happy they were being used.

Whether it was talking too long on the telephone (Shannon's mom also told me that Shannon got negative conduct marks on her school report card for "talking" too much in class) or sneaking a bottle of wine, our handicapped friends showed a complete spectrum of both good and bad traits. In other words, they were just like any other group of teens. It was certainly not the first time a group of teens had pulled the old wine caper on a church retreat.

We were not mad, although a little embarrassed we had not caught them in the act. I did have ten guys who were a little ticked because they had to help five big inebriated blind fellows to their cabins. I told Craig he was in charge of that detail, and while they did that, Chuck and I put out the fire. By the time I had finished, everyone seemed to have made it to their cabins. I headed for my tent.

The "Wino Five" might have caught me by surprise, but I was not so naïve as to think that the night's activities were over just because the schedule said lights out at 12 AM. While the campfire shenanigans belonged to the campers, the rest of the night's mischief would be perpetrated by the counselors.

I was comforted by two thoughts, only one of which was a sure thing. First, there was always the faint hope that a few might actually be afraid of what lay out there on the edge of the Haunted Woods in the Piankatank night. I didn't put too much faith in that wish, but I was confident that the counselors would abide by our unwritten "fifty-percent rule."

It was verbally stated and completely understood that, at any one time, each cabin would keep half of the counselors inside with the campers. This rule kind of evolved from the counselors themselves during the first years. Each time something happened, they would truthfully assure me that half of them had been "on duty," so to speak. I thought this was probably the best I could hope for, and so I made it an official rule. Considering the number of helpers, the fifty-percent rule meant that we generally still had a one-to-one ratio in the cabins at any given time.

Ministry with the Handicapped

Thirty-six million Americans, or one of six, have physical, mental or emotional disabilities. This is one of the largest minorities in America today and one that respects no age, race, sex or social class. Anyone can become disabled. These "disabled" are people who have abilities and can make an important contribution to our society.

The Department of Christian Social Ministries of The Home Mission Board helps the church open its doors and extend its arms to welcome those with mental, physical and/or psychologically

handicapped conditions. The healing grace of the community of faith must be available to these.

Ministry with handicapped persons is through state conventions, associations and local churches. The objectives of this ministry are to provide opportunities of involvement for those who are physically disadvantaged and to help the church to be sensitive and responsible in meeting needs.

Determine Needs

❏ Contact agencies of employment and vocational rehabilitation for suggestions and information about existing needs.
❏ Contact private organizations which minister to people with severly crippling diseases.

Steve Hayes with Edrick in a 1970s Home Missions Board brochure

74

19
A Scream in the Dark

*B*ecause we had taken such a large number of helpers on this retreat, there were a couple of sleeping quarters that housed only volunteers. I was fully aware that this was only asking for trouble, but I had no other real choice. Having only one or two campers in a sleeping area did not change things in that respect. Better to have most of the cabins filled up with "responsibility." One of the all-counselor accommodations was a big tent platform on top of the hill, close to the upper restroom facilities. Rene Cantu, one of the three Cantus on the retreat, was in this tent, along with her sister Stephanie and several others.

~

Stephanie, who possessed great actress abilities, once used her talent to get me big time. This was at the urging of Pete, Steve, Doug, and Bill Bowman. The four of them were at a lock-in, from which I had to leave early because I was refereeing football games the next morning. At the time, I had just started dating a very good-looking lady. We were going out a couple of nights later, and I had made the grievous mistake of telling my friends about the upcoming date.

At four in the morning, I was awakened by the telephone. I walked in a daze to the room where my phone was and somehow got the receiver to my ear. It sounded like Lynn. I was completely fooled by the voice. In fact, the person on the other end was so convincing, I really thought my new friend felt it important to call me in the wee hours of the morning, simply to break a date. (Please don't make the mistake of thinking I was used to having a lot of dates broken. In order to have that problem, you have to have a lot of dates to begin with!) I probably would have stood her up if Bill and the rest had not started laughing in the background. I did get my revenge later.

The girls in the tent had stayed up a while talking but were now ready to get some sleep. This was not because they wanted to behave, though. They had plans for my car later in the night and could afford to catch a few Zs in the meantime.

Rene turned off the Coleman lantern, their only source of light, and slipped into her sleeping bag. She let the events of the day play through her mind and a smile passed over her lips as she thought of the mischief they had planned for later. Then, safe in the knowledge that they had set the alarm, she began to drift off to sleep. All was quiet for the next five minutes. Then, suddenly Rene's bed came alive. Its first tentative movement was a short sliding motion. Rene opened her eyes, thinking the bed's movement had been her imagination. It wasn't.

Still somewhat groggy with sleep, Rene's mind popped back to her last hospital visit. Could this be act two? That night she had fought a battle with a pack of attack balloons. It had been a tough hospital visit for Rene. First, she had mistakenly filled out her dinner menu, thinking it had been for an entire week. Luckily, her mom and I had come and helped her eat the abundance of food. Then, later that night, a bouquet of helium balloons had literally descended upon her. She awoke in a drug-induced fog (hospital-administered), fighting off the strings and rubber spheres bouncing around her head.

In the tent, things quickly got worse than the hospital room battle. A lot worse. What started as a slow slide escalated into a jerking motion, and then, amid Rene's screams, the bed lunged toward the back of the tent. Rene continued screaming as one of the legs dropped off the tent platform, leaving the bed and Rene in a somewhat precarious tilt. By now, every girl in the tent was screaming. Becky Russell stopped long enough to reach out toward Rene's bed and shout, "What's going on?"

Becky had no sooner gotten the words out of her mouth than the tent flaps opened and a louder-pitched screech emanated from outside. That was immediately followed by several streams of cold water flowing into the tent. This brought on a renewed chorus of screams from those inside. By the time the girls realized they were being assaulted by buckets of water, the culprits had dropped the flaps and sunk into the night.

Meanwhile, back at my tent, five of us were feeling around for our shoes even as the first scream faded into the night. "I think we're on," I said. "I guess we need to make some sort of effort to find out what's happening." This was going to result in a loss of sleep while accomplishing nothing.

Still, I was the director, and that called for some kind of response. This wasn't totally unexpected. Naturally, all of us had been sleeping with our clothes on. We laced up our boots and headed for the sound of the machine-gun screams. By the time we got to the tent, things had settled down a bit. Rene was threatening to kill Doug and "that little Petey!" We put her bed back on the platform and told them to try and get some sleep. At that moment, Ailor spotted a single file of dark figures sneaking through the trees in front of the tent, heading toward the campfire area. We shouted the customary command:

"Stop! Right now, guys! We mean it!"

The customary shout was followed by the customary response. They took off! We started in pursuit, knowing they would not stop. We soon lost sight of them in the more heavily wooded area, but we kept on in the general direction we had last seen them heading. We came to the edge of the tree line and stepped out into the archery field. It was still an extremely dark and moonless night. I could not see anyone, but now I had a more urgent problem. I told Sinclair to tell our crew to hold up while I took a leak. At this time, I almost got my revenge.

I walked back into the woods, up to a tree surrounded by some heavy foliage. Little did I know that this was the spot where Pete and Steve had decided to hide. They immediately realized what was going to happen but did not want to give their position away. Fortunately for the duo, I stopped short of their actual positions and my stream of water did not reach them. (What a shame!)

I came back to the edge of the tree line and saw our enforcement team standing near one of the archery targets. They were shining their lights across the field toward the trees on the opposite side of the field.

"Mike," Ailor whispered, "look out toward where our lights are shining, but don't expect to see anything because nobody is over there."

"Sure," I replied, not quite understanding. Nothing really fazed me about these types of encounters. But hearing the question in my reply, Ailor went on. "We are trying the old 'look-the-other-way' ploy. Chuck saw several of them hide behind the big tree next to the dining hall back door." The tree was in front of us but to the right of where our combined lights were shining.

"How many?" I asked. (Dumb question. What difference did it make?)

"We don't know, but this is what we're going to do. We'll keep our lights trained on the same spot at the edge of the woods. Then we'll walk at a diagonal across the field toward that spot. When we reach the closest point to the tree, I yell, and we rush them."

"Great plan," said Sinclair, as he led out, followed by the rest of us.

I'm thinking, even as we commenced our clever plan of deception, *Why even bother?* If we caught them, all I'd do is tell them to get back to their cabins. They would say OK, but who knew if they would comply. Besides, this line of thought was probably speculative. What *would* happen is that they will take off again. Still, they needed to be yelled at a little. They had gone too close to the edge of acceptable behavior by pulling Rene's bed off the platform, though that was probably not intentional.

I didn't want to admit to myself the other reason we were chasing them. It had become kind of a game, and we were trapped in it. Still, most of all, I wanted to get "whatever" done quickly and back to my own bunk. Over the years, I had become fatalistic. The volunteers were going to carry out their schemes each night. I considered those events as I considered Freight Train's nightly snoring. *Go ahead, but let me get to sleep first.*

I was mulling over all these thoughts in my head when Ailor let out a scream equal to any we had heard that night. (Well, if anyone in this camp was still asleep, it would be a miracle.) I was so startled, I found myself running a little behind the other four, as we made a beeline for the tree. From behind the tree, cries of "Let's get the heck out of here!" or something close to that, were followed by several guys making a dash from our left to our right.

Yes, they had opted for possibility number two: run away! ("Run away…." Now where have we heard that before? Oh, yes, quoting *Monty Py-*

thon and the Holy Grail movie was a favorite of camp counselors in those days, especially Paul Wygal and Bill Sinclair.) We were in pretty good shape ourselves, but these guys were both young and in good shape. No way we were going to catch them. Still, we pursued. After all, that was another unwritten camp rule. We were, to be sure, the authorities on this night, and the authorities were expected to give chase. Otherwise, what fun was it to be almost captured!

I was still trailing the posse as we ran past the tree. The "rabbits" were flying across the field in front of the pavilion. For some reason, I glanced to my left. There, next to the tree, I saw Doug Cantu. He had not moved when the others took off, obviously hoping we would run by him without noticing. I made a quick turn to my left and yelled, "Stay right where you are!"

Doug knew the answer to that statement. For the second time that night, he took to his heels. By the time I made my running turn to the left, Doug had gotten to the corner of the dining hall. He had also managed to put an obstacle between us. I had to slow down in order to navigate the clotheslines, which ran out from the building to poles around the tree. By the time I got to the edge of the building, I could see no one.

I kept on till I got to the road that led into camp. Off to my right, in the big field, I could see some shapes walking around. That would be Ailor and company. I knew Doug could not have gone in that direction without being seen. I stepped onto the road and turned left. The infirmary loomed on my right, a few yards ahead. That was a definite hiding place possibility.

The outside light was on as we had requested. Inside, it was dark and quiet. That meant absolutely nothing. Every person in the camp, with the exception of the girls in the tent, would be an ally of those we were chasing. I walked around the building, following the beam of my flashlight. Doug was nowhere to be seen. Coming back up the other side, I paused at an open window. Listen as I might, I could hear nothing inside. Still, it was the only thing that made sense. Finally, from inside came Kelly Johnson's voice. It sounded a bit too surprised and innocent.

"Who's out there?"

I decided to try a ruse that had actually worked one time on a youth retreat. I had suckered out Jimmy Ailor and one of his many girlfriends. They were hiding in a building that had no interior lights. I had been sent to find·

the two, as it was past lights out. (Lights out in the occupied cabins, that is!) I didn't have a clue as to whether they were in the building or not, and there was no way to find out, as I didn't have a flashlight with me at the time. I shouted with feigned confidence, "Come on out, you two. Jimmy, it's time to head back!" I do not know who was more surprised when Jim and his girl-friend walked out. *What the heck*, I said to myself, *perhaps I'll get lucky again.*

"Kelly, it's me, Mike. Tell Doug to come out. He needs to get back to the cabin with his kids!"

The girls inside—Kelly, Jeri Hudson, Donna Jo, and Kelly Williams, shouted out in unison:

"Doug is *not* in here!"

"You woke us up!"

"Go to bed and leave us alone!"

Well, they had called my bluff. I certainly wasn't about to go inside and search. I did make a mental note to be sure and wake them up first thing in the morning. I figured I could walk a little ways away and wait to see if anyone came out of the building. However, by this time, I was more interested in getting a little sleep than in catching Doug or anyone else. I walked back up the road and found my friends sitting in the pavilion. We traded war stories, the gist of which was that none of us had caught anyone. We then decided we had done our duty as mature(?) leaders, and so off we went to rack it.

Meanwhile, back in the infirmary, justice was being served at that very moment. Even as I had been standing outside the window, Doug had been following in his mind the journey of at least two insects crawling up his leg. His only prayer was that they were not spiders. His arms, legs, and stomach burned in a dozen skinned spots, the results of his earlier dive through the infirmary window. Ten feet away was a well-equipped medical cabinet. If only I would leave.

Then things got a little worse when one of the critters crawling up his leg decided to stop for a bit of dinner, perhaps "leg of Doug." A moment after I moved on, Doug decided he could take it no longer. He gently reached down and flicked off his tormentors. The girls pulled him from beneath the bed, and using their flashlights, they began to search for cuts and bruises. A half hour later, Doug was able to cautiously open the door and sneak back to his cabin. He crept slowly across the soccer field, keeping low to the ground.

And while he was busy scratching insect bites, those of us in the tent were snoozing in our bunks.

The rest of the night passed quietly, if not uneventfully.

Above: Ann Laferriere and Jeri Hudson eat steamed crabs caught by the campers.

Right: Belinda Crowley, another out-of-state Smishy, helps her camper begin to get over a fear of the water.

Right: Daily Press caption reads, "Counselor Marianne Williams... literally holds a conversation in her hands."

Below: Marianne, whom I called "Murry Ann"

20

Marianne in the Morning

Mornings were always invigorating and beautiful at Camp Piankatank. One of the advantages of sleeping in a tent is that you get to wake up to the first rays of the sunrise. You also get the full effect of the songbirds' morning chorus, high in the trees above you—truly one of those special moments God gives to us each day.

I sat up in my cot and gave words of greetings to my companions. Ailor pulled a pillow over his head, and Sinclair mumbled something unintelligible. Chuck Paul, Larry Van Wyngarden, and Dean Jernigan just slept on, oblivious to this beautiful dawn.

There were two things that made a Piankatank morning very special to me. One was that I got to give the official wake-up call for all of the cabins, tents, *and* the infirmary! Since most of the counselors had probably been out to all hours of the night, they would be fast asleep when I arrived. This was one of the times I felt a little sadistic because I loved it so much.

However, the wake-up call was the second priority on these mornings. The first thing was to seek out a steaming cup of black coffee. From the looks of my tent mates this morning, it was a safe bet that I would get the first cup out of the pot.

At least I did not have to go and get the cooks this morning. That had allowed me another half hour of sleep. At this time in the morning, a half hour of sleep was equal to an hour of sleep any other time of the day. Both cooks lived near the camp, but neither of them could any longer drive. They were in their eighties. Sometimes they could get a ride on weekends, and sometimes they needed help from the camp staff.

The meals at camp were not always the best in the world, but there was always plenty for seconds. And for me at least, the food was good enough to warrant seconds. However, these two ladies had two special talents that made up for any limitations. One is that they were as good as gold to our campers. They added to the retreats with their humor and conversation. Their second gift was that they could make a great pot of coffee. Coffee is more important than any meal, especially at breakfast. Believe it!

The cooks also did the little extra things you requested. The year before, during our crabbing time, which usually did not yield much, we had hit the jackpot. On Saturday, the campers had caught several dozen crabs. We asked the ladies if they would steam them for us. Seafood they knew. Dinner that night was a real treat.

I pulled on a pair of shoes, leaving my socks off. That was one little trick I had learned over the years. The early morning dew was always heavy. By the time I finished my rounds, this pair of shoes would be soaked, but I would not waste a pair of dry socks.

The morning walk to the kitchen and coffee urn was always an adventure in itself. It was then that I usually learned what else had gone on in the night. This stroll turned up all sorts of flotsam from the latest encounters of ships that passed in the night. I was curious about one thing, and so I detoured to the campfire area first. The fire was completely out, as I had expected. Off a ways from the ashes, I found what I was looking for. It seemed that Thunderbird was the drink of preference the previous night. I picked up the two empty bottles and headed for the trash can at the pavilion.

On the way, I stopped and added a discarded sleeping bag to my morning collection. Later, I found out it was left from Marianne's late-night adventure. Ralph Talton and a couple of others had burst into her cabin sometime after I fell asleep. While half a dozen deaf girls applauded, they threw the sleeping bag over her head and carried Marianne off into the night. Now, for Marianne, from the flat state of Texas, any woods are dark and deep. In actuality, she was deposited only thirty yards from the cabin, but it had taken her quite a while to find her way back.

~

A word about Marianne, or "Murry Ann," as I called her. She came to us from Texas, and we liked her so much that she became the first out-of-state "Smishy" (summer missionary) that I asked back for the next summer. She has probably stayed more in touch with me over the years than any of my other out-of-state Smishies. That is, if you do not count Diane Sexton Seward and Susan Riley Miller, who stayed on in this area. Diane became a youth director for one of our churches and is still here. Susan married a guy from one of our churches. They moved away for a while and then came back for a spell, during which time she also became a youth director.

This is not to say that a lot of them didn't keep in touch. However, Marianne, Dee Dee Hartless, and Stel Washburn have written the most interesting letters over the years. One of the nice things about Marianne's letters was that they represented a microcosm of the typical life of a Smishy. Her letters contained a wide variety of topics, but almost every one included some comments on her most favorite subject: boys.

When Marianne first came to Virginia, she was being pursued by two guys. One was a long-time boyfriend named Van, who Jimmy George, Craig Waddell, and I called her "Main Man Van," and who was also a "Vantastic" fellow.

She was also the romantic focus of a contemporary Christian singer I had actually heard of, Tim Sheppard. To be honest, I thought she was putting me on about Tim and the fact that he was chasing her all over the nation. When Tim eventually arrived in Newport News, I had to accept the truth. He was following her like a puppy dog. He played the piano at a small church service, where the Smishies were in charge of the program. For Jimmy George, it was the highlight of his singing career—a professional musician on piano as Jimmy sang "Rise Again."

Marianne eventually dumped those two guys and married a gentleman who works with the hearing impaired. They now have five kids. I still hear from her around the time of my birthday each year.

As I said, we liked her so much that we brought her back for a second year. She would have to fly in from the Bahamas (living the tough missionary life, obviously).

One night in May, I was at home when I got a phone call. It was from a complete stranger. He told me he was a ham radio operator, and he was helping to patch through a call for me. It was from one yacht, which had a small set, to another yacht, which had a more powerful transmitter. The larger yacht had contacted the radio operator in my town. I was pretty excited and didn't know who it could be until I heard Marianne's voice. She was sailing the Bahamas with her family and had called to let me know what flight she would be coming in on.

Left: Marcia and Heather Moore

Below: Chuck Paul instructs our counselors in proper use of the paddle.

22
Poetic Justice

*A*rriving at the pavilion, I dropped the wine bottles in the trash and laid the sleeping bag on a table. Then I looked out toward the road and saw what had been the main activity of the night.

My car. It was a classic.

No, *my car* was not a classic. The prank was a classic. My car sat in the morning mist, sporting a beautiful coat of toilet paper, leaves, vines, and all sorts of other natural decorations. Now, my car had been decorated dozens of times over the years. (Once I got back from a Florida diving trip and found both my car and my front door decorated with TP, bells, and other wedding odds and ends. That was compliments of Pete, Scott, and Steve. For the next month, tenants at my apartment complex kept congratulating me on my marriage.)

But this morning it was, I believe, the best it had ever looked. I knew it would not be fair to clean it up until everyone had seen it. I took a couple of photos and headed for the cafeteria.

Well, there was one other time when my car was done up in classic style, and this time for a large audience. I walked out of the movie theater with a date—please no comments—late one freezing evening. As we exited the lobby door, my date laughed and pointed at a well-decorated car in the parking lot. She remarked that someone had a bit of cleaning up to do. I didn't even have to double-check where she was pointing. Burnette, Smith, and Millar were in town, and I even suspected they were somewhere in the parking lot. They were. Toilet paper was blowing in the wind, and the windshield was covered with Vaseline, as were the door handles.

Later, I discovered the reason my car was so well adorned at camp this morning. Turned out, two different groups of counselors had planned to carry out the same prank. The first group hit shortly after I went to bed for the second time that night. The next group, which included the girls on the hill, arrived later and simply added to what had been done by the first group. It was the second group that added the vines and branches. At least one person was later to regret that action.

I finally arrived at the kitchen and poured my first morning cup of coffee. I stood, chatting with the cooks, while enjoying that cup. Then I poured a second cup and headed for my first wake-up call—the infirmary and sweet revenge.

I softly opened the front door and stepped inside, careful not to make any noise. The front door opened into a main room. Here were the medical supplies and a table. There was another room directly behind this one, which had a couple of cots. Off to the left of this room was a small shower. This shower was the nicest perk about staying in the infirmary. It was the only one in the camp with really hot water. The rest of the showers were only lukewarm at best.

To the left of the room I was standing in was another bedroom with four cots. This was the room into which Doug had made his running dive. The girls were now fast asleep. Good! I stood still for a few seconds to savor the moment and to make sure they were soundly sleeping. I moved to the open door. Then, I flipped on the lights and, at the top of my lungs, shouted, "Hey, girls! It's a beautiful morning. Time to rise and shine!"

"Haywood, I'm going to—" I made a hasty retreat before Kelly Williams could get out the words "kill you!" Besides, I had other cabins waiting for me.

When I walked up the road past the cafeteria, I saw a few bodies beginning to make their way slowly across the field toward the two bathrooms on either side of the pool. In the early morning mist, their slow movements reminded me of a 1950s zombie movie. Weird, but not scary. Some of these figures were holding onto the elbow of the person in front. After a few words with these early morning risers, I knew there were still many victims waiting for me at each stop.

By the time I had sung a song for each of the cabins, I saw a group of the guys, standing in the road drinking coffee. (For some strange reason, my singing seems to wake people up rather than put them to sleep. Except for the song "Woolly Bully," which Tammy George loves to hear me sing. It brings tears to her eyes.) I went through the kitchen for a refill and then walked out to join them.

The topic of conversation was my car. Ailor and Chuck were discussing who the decorators might have been. I mentioned that it was not out of the question for the whole camp to be involved.

Dean Jernigan remarked that it was a very good job and then went on to say, "Mike, you know, no one would ever realize just how dirty your car is by the way it looks now."
Ailor and Chuck agreed that the culprit would probably never be identified.

Sinclair, who had been looking at the car intently the whole time, spoke up with a laugh. "Oh, I'm not so sure of that. I think we'll be able to discover the identity of at least one of them."

"How are we going to be able to do that?" I asked.

"Well, now, it may take a few days, but it could happen. Depends on the person. Perhaps we won't know."

Ailor said, "OK, I give up. How are we going to find out, or possibly not find out?"

Bill led us toward the car. It was a beaut. Toilet paper, vines, and flower decor abounded. Bill pointed to one of the vines draped across the hood.

"Know what that is?" he asked no one in particular.

"Poison ivy!" exclaimed Chuck. "Haywood, someone put poison ivy on your car!"

Bill continued, "Now, perhaps they knew they were immune and did it on purpose. But I'm willing to bet you that in the dark they didn't know what they had gotten hold of. The possibility still exists, of course, that they didn't know it was poison ivy and are immune to it. So, it's only a maybe."

All the while, I was thinking, *Surely the Lord will not let this bit of poetic justice slip by.* Someone was soon going to learn about living with the consequences of their actions. For the second time that morning, I felt a bit sadistic. This was going to be fun.

"Perhaps we can find out a little sooner, like at breakfast," I ventured.
"Look, I'll announce this in the dining hall, and we can all look for signs of

dismay. It might work."

We decided it was worth the chance. However, never did I dream that the culprit would be sitting right across the table from me. Pete was sitting beside me, and I kind of wondered if it had been him or perhaps Burnette. Halfway through breakfast, I stood up and told the group that I had an announcement to make. As soon as the words "poison ivy" came out of my mouth, Stel's face dropped to the floor.

Pete looked at Stel and pronounced his current favorite epitaph, "You've been crispified!"

She made it through the weekend in good shape. But on Monday night, Ralph Talton and I saw her at Friendly's, and she told us she had been to the doctor that day for a shot. I loved it.

Well, the night was over, and it was time to start the day. If the night belonged to the counselors, then the day belonged totally to the campers. Later, I found out that the night had also belonged to some of the campers. I learned that Stel and Josie's cabin had gotten around the fifty-percent rule by the simple but effective method of taking their vision-impaired girls with them to help decorate my car!

Top: Wesley shows the love of God.

Above: Paul Wygal shows patience in teaching.

Left: Karen Paschal instructs our out-of-state Smishy. Sometimes we taught the campers and sometimes we taught each other.

Opposite: My car, decorated with TP and poison ivy

91

Above: The girl in the bandana suffered from a brain tumor. Darlene Shanabrook is her counselor.

Below left: Troy Hicks *Below right:* David Cromer, Pete Burnette, and I attach balloons to the target so that the visually impaired can hear the sound of the balloon popping when they hit the target.

22
Perpetual Motion

One of the more interesting aspects of our retreats was the fact that everything and everybody always appeared to be in a state of total confusion. Well, perhaps there really was a little confusion, but things always worked themselves out.

Actually, at the camper/counselor level, there was no confusion. One of our main goals was to let the campers do whatever they most enjoyed. Sure, there were times when I made everyone try a specific activity, so they could decide if they liked it or not. Ironically, there were times when the campers liked the activity a lot more than the counselors. This often happened during the canoeing and was especially true if neither the camper nor the counselor were very good at it. In those cases, the counselors had to do most of the work, while the camper kind of paddled half-heartedly and enjoyed the trip. Those canoes often headed in a little early.

The counselor would say they wanted to try something else, but when I asked, the camper was always ready for more canoeing. Many a time, I pushed a canoe back out into the river while the sore-armed counselor begged for mercy and the camper shouted for joy. I would just smile and say "Enjoy!"

So, while there were a few periods of planned group activities, most of the time was spent following the campers' lead. There was one major exception. The pool was only open at certain times. That was because some of our campers, if allowed, would spend every waking moment at the pool.

This morning, following breakfast, groups could choose from canoeing, sailing, crabbing, kayaking, fishing, archery, hiking, or just walking around. The only two things they could not do was swim or go back to the cabins. They could stay at any of these activities as long as they wanted—

spending the entire period at one or hitting several for shorter periods of time. Canoeing and kayaking had the advantage of a built-in second adventure. These groups could go to the island for a hike, head upstream a mile or so and hunt for fossilized shells, or both.

As a rule, the only sport that was not well attended during free activity times was archery. This was noticeably true during a very hot weekend. Even then, we could count on two or three groups to be participating at any one time. This particular weekend, there was a large group that decided to try archery before the sun got up too high. Since I usually spent this time walking around and snapping pictures, I decided to go to the archery range first.

We tried to make every event at camp as safe as possible. Obviously, archery was one of the activities in which we took special precautions. If the counselors were not on top of the situation, a major accident could result. Cliff Bowen was in charge of the archery this morning. I tried to rotate activity assignments so that everyone got to spend some time at all of them. Cliff, the Chief of Police in Poquoson (now retired), had a special advantage at this spot. No matter where he stood, he was tall enough to see what was going on at each target.

The balloons had already been tied to the targets. The sound of bursting balloons would serve as a reinforcement for the visually impaired when they hit the target. At the start, volunteers instructed each of the campers on how to string a bow. For the hearing-impaired kids, this was not too great a learning challenge. Since most of them were very young, their greatest challenge was in being able to bend the bow. The visually impaired had to take a little more time just to get the feel of a bow. Then they would listen to the patient instructions on how to hold it while fitting the string into the notch.

As in all our activities, the campers would have to learn to go through the whole sequence, not just shoot a few arrows with someone else holding the bow. Earlier, when they had first arrived at the field, the campers were taken to the targets so they could familiarize themselves with the receiving end of the arrow. When all this was done, the groups moved away to a point, which was a little closer than where one would normally stand. The next step was learning to place and hold the arrow. When this was accomplished, the command was given to commence firing.

By the time you get there, most of the hearing impaired have grown impatient, waiting for their sightless companions to get the hang of things. When the firing command was given, this group of young archers would immediately unleash a barrage of arrows. Undaunted by early misses, they would continue in rapid-fire order until they began to hit the target.

Working with the visually impaired on the archery range was somewhat akin to firing salvos from a naval vessel. We used the concept of ranging in on the target as we told our friends where their last arrows landed. Then the helpers gave instructions for correcting their aim as the campers readied their second salvo.

I drifted over to where Monica Morse, Jeri Hudson, and Denise Harris were talking with Ruth and Belinda. The five of them made a great team. All were very talkative, though not in a loud way. The way they worked together made you think they had known each other for years.

There was no better example of love and mutual respect among youth than shown by these girls. Monica was a member of one of our churches and had been a big help at several events over the years. She was fun to have around and she fit in perfectly with the Group.

Both Jeri and Denise worked as part of my summer mission team. Denise was a pretty blonde girl, who was a lot more attractive than she thought she was. This fact helped me get her to work with our Smishy team. I wanted her to be involved because, like Jeri, she filled all the requirements. Both loved the Lord, loved working with others, and were able to put up with the team's offbeat sense of humor. However, when I first wrote and asked her about participating, she wrote back from college that she was undecided as to what she should do the coming summer.

I then played my ace card—a photo I had taken of Denise and Lynne Everhart. It was taken at the retreat the year before and showed the two girls getting ready to take their camper out in a canoe. Both looked great, Denise in a two-piece. But Denise didn't think she looked great. In fact, she hated the photograph. I simply told her in a letter that if she didn't work as a Smishy the next summer, I would put eight-by-ten copies of that photo all over town.

I got an immediate letter of acceptance. Things worked out brilliantly. I got to keep the photo, and Denise became a Smishy. (Denise, I still have that photo and you still look great in it. And I kept my word. It is not plastered all over town. There is only a four-by-six up on my office wall!)

Written on the back of the envelope of the return letter from Denise:

PS. The picture threat was real cute, Mike!

"Good shot!" Denise told Belinda, while giving me a smile that said, *I think we know what we are doing here.*

Jeri's smile matched Denise's as she put a hand on Ruth's shoulder. "You have a good grip on the bow. Your shot was so strong that the arrow went over the top of the target and slightly to the left," she informed Ruth. "Mike's here now, so let's show him what we girls can do."

"Watch me, Mike," Ruth called out. "After I'm done, we'll teach you." She fired again.

Jeri exclaimed, "Almost! Ruth, that was at the perfect height. Just a bit off to the right this time. You want to come back just a bit."

Ruth's friend Belinda was also finding the range. "Come on, Mike, we can even show *you* how to do this."

"No way," Monica said. "Mike is a wimp!" (I always commanded the deepest respect from all my volunteers.)

Pop went a balloon. Ruth had hit the bullseye. "Hey, Mike, let me see you do that!"

I begged off. If I tried and missed, I would never hear the end of it. Having taken a few pictures, I wished them well and headed off. As I was leaving, I could hear similar instructions all down the line.

"Lower, lower, and a little to your left."

"Too much. You need to come back some."

"Whenever you're ready."

"Good shot! You almost hit the target."

These directions continued until the burst of a balloon would signify to one of the blind students that they had hit something. After being told what area of the target they hit, it was back to another arrow to try again. When all the arrows had been expended, it was time for Cliff to give the command to lay down the bows. This was a critical command before going to retrieve the spent arrows. You never could fully trust the younger hearing-impaired kids not to let it fly if they happened to have one more at their disposal. Everyone fanned out and began to collect the arrows, which lay anywhere from a few feet in front of the archers to many yards behind the targets. Then it was back on the firing line. Soon, both campers and helpers would be sharing time with the bows. I never did remember to ask Denise and Jeri if they measured up to Ruth's and Belinda's standards.

The last thing I saw reminded me of a conversation I'd had with a friend a few weeks earlier. I had been talking about the retreat, and he asked if it was not dangerous to put a bow and arrow in the hands of "blind people." I replied, truthfully, that there was one danger. Many of my volunteers have had their pride hurt when the campers start hitting bullseyes while the volunteers couldn't even hit the targets.

John Hogge had just fired one wildly over the top of the target, but I didn't think it would hurt his self-image too much. Since his camper was in a wheelchair, John was firing from ground level in order to figure out the same shooting angle as his friend. As for me—well, I told you. I walked away from Ruth's challenge to shoot against her!

I'm enclosing a picture of our two boys.... I find it hard to believe that my summers at the blind/deaf camp and as a summer missionary are so far behind me.... (Wow. Do you ever feel like you are getting older? I think of you as part Peter Pan...never quite losing the child.) You asked about our memories, and I have been thinking hard.... I remember realizing how truly "brave" those kids were...allowing teenagers to lead them into the wild where nothing was familiar.... And archery, as the blind students made bullseyes, I made bruises on my arm.

—Jeri

Above: Bob Moore instructs a camper. Note the double hose regulator he is using.

Below left: Jim George lifeguards. Many of the counselors took my lifesaving course, which really helped out a lot.

Below right: Bo Micheille checks out Karen Watts, while Karen lifeguards.

23
Blood in the Water

I should say a word at this point about the dangers of these activities, and how well we fared in our efforts to do things in a safe manner. Let me explain by telling about one of our accidents. It occurred in the swimming pool early one Saturday afternoon.

A group of vision-impaired campers and their counselors got into a splashing contest. They were close to the side of the pool, when one of the visually impaired turned his head away from the group. He hit the side of the pool and cut a fair-sized gash in his forehead. We got him out of the pool and cleaned up the wound at the infirmary. We could tell it needed stitches, so we sent him off to town to see a doctor, which the camp used. He returned about an hour later with three stitches. He was back in the water at the next session, being careful to stay away from the sides and keeping the bandage dry.

That was one of only two times in twenty years that we had to have a kid checked out by a doctor. (This includes all events, not just the retreats.) Certainly, we have had bumps and bruises. Campers have walked into trees or the sides of bunks. We have not been perfect. Once, we even had a kid hit another in the head with a baseball bat. It was an accident. Waylon, who *wasn't* visually impaired, didn't look where he was going and walked right where the other kid was swinging at a baseball. The other kid wasn't visually impaired either!

But these are the types of accidents that occasionally happen at any camp. I think we have done remarkably well, and that is a testament to the young counselors who staffed all our events over the years.

I mention the pool incident because there were two humorous events associated with the gashed head. When the accident first occurred, there was a lot of blood in the water. Swimming by were a number of both vision- and hearing-impaired campers. It was rather funny to watch two opposite reactions. Several blind kids continued to swim unknowingly through the blood-tainted water, while the deaf kids vacated the pool like they had seen a shark.

The second humorous sidelight involved Cliff Bowen at the infirmary. Cliff had just gone through a volunteer emergency-room helper course at a local hospital. It was fun to listen to him use jargon like "irrigate the cut" (wash it out) and "let's close the wound" (put a bandage on it). Hey, Cliff was on the right track. He later married Cindy, a nurse.

We learned another thing about Cliff while on this retreat. Steve Burnette had ridden to camp in a station wagon full of girls. Steve later related that the girls were talking about how well—or how not so well—Cliff kissed. It so happened that everyone in the car had been out with Cliff at least once, and they had finally gotten together for a chance to compare notes. We used to have a saying that Cliff did not have flames—he had matches!

Like with archery, people sometimes ask whether we should do certain activities with the handicapped. The person asking the question is usually concerned about the possibility of one of the campers getting hurt. And it is a valid question with a valid answer. My reply is that they are right. Someone could get hurt. However, it is also true that a group of youth, who can see and hear, stand a chance of getting hurt at camp, or playing sports, or any other activity. And we do not stop them from trying the activities.

I have always felt that our visually, hearing, and mentally challenged have the right to try the same things we do, with the same risks. (Not greater risk, but the same.) At times, all of us take reasonable risks. I also like to point out that the greatest risk we take with our friends is not the activities we embark upon. It is going out on the nation's highways to get there. Now that is a risk. Still, our camp safety record speaks for itself.

Left: Trey Daniels and Rob Young

Below: Joe Paul Bragg in the *Daily Press*

Above: Beth Neal and Molley Thomas pose for me, while two of the hearing-impaired guys check out their poses!

Below: Two campers with Lori Blankenship, Kelly Gray (out-of-state Smishy), John Kirtley, Scott Millar, and John Whitsel

24
An Invigorating Shower

*M*eanwhile, back at camp, the door to the infirmary opened slowly and quietly. It was mid-morning, and no one was inside, except for the person taking a shower. Jimmy George had waited for this perfect moment, and now it was his. He could hear the shower going full force in the back room. Jimmy was one of the veterans who knew this trick of the trade.

The shower stall in the infirmary was cleaner and had warmer water than any of the other facilities. It was also the only shower where you stood a chance of enjoying the experience without being disturbed. Therefore, those of us in the know would try to get away unseen and take a leisurely shower. It always felt good on a Saturday morning. Jimmy had been waiting, not to use the shower himself, but for me to take advantage of this luxury. Now he was ready to get his revenge for whatever I had done to him lately. (That could have been most anything.) Later, Jimmy told me that he could visualize the look on my face when a bucket of cold water came over the top of the shower curtain and cascaded down my body.

The plan was a good one. The infirmary shower was fantastic in comparison to the others, but even here the water was not exactly hot. The cold water at Camp Piankatank is just that—cold! Jimmy found the biggest bucket around and, hoping the shower would keep running, filled it up from the tap in the other room. The shower ran on. Jimmy then tippy-toed into the back room where he pulled off a perfect attack. Every drop of water made it over the top, splashing down into the shower and onto its occupant. He had only to wait a split second before he heard an ear-piercing scream. At that point, he decided a quick retreat was in order.

I had left the archery range and was walking past the cafeteria toward the road when I heard a door slam and the sounds of laughter coming up the road to my left. As I rounded the side of the cafeteria and stepped into the road, I came face to face with a quick-stepping Jimmy George. I didn't know the reason at that moment, but the look on Jimmy's face was priceless.

"You're not in the shower?" he said with that same stupid look on his face.

"No," I replied, "But I am heading that way if you want to walk with me."

"Perhaps you'd best not go over that way right now. Let's walk over to the pavilion for a second." I followed Jimmy to a spot where we could see the front door of the infirmary. Along the way, Jimmy filled me in on his earlier encounter. Now he just wanted to know who he had splashed.

We only had to wait about five minutes before the regular summer camp director walked out. He wasn't smiling. Jimmy decided to go with me down to the waterfront, where he could hook up with the campers.

At that moment, someone came running up and told me that I needed to get down to the river—fast. There had been an accident. Donna Strother had fallen down the steps that led to the waterfront area. No word on whether she had been hurt or not. Jimmy and I started off on a run to the beach. The stairs are long and steep. A fall could cause a serious injury—just what we didn't need. The irony, of course, was that Donna wasn't visually impaired. She was one of my veteran volunteers.

By the time we made it to the bottom of the stairs, Donna was sitting up, rubbing her elbows and shins. It turned out that the only thing hurt was Donna's pride. She explained that she was leading Edna to the top of the stairs with no problems. However, when she got on the steps themselves, she had been paying so much attention to Edna that she forgot what her own feet were doing.

Donna had backed down a couple of steps and told Edna just how steep the stairway was. She made sure her camper had her hands on the railing. When Edna was situated, Donna turned to walk in front. As she stepped down, her shoe got caught on the edge of one of the runners. The next thing Donna knew, she was tumbling down.

There are some thirty steps going down to the landing, and Donna managed to hit each and every one of them, finally coming to a stop at the landing on her bottom. By the time Donna had recovered and was sitting up, Edna had made it down safely on her own.

⮑

The waterfront, as always, was a hubbub of activity. People were moving in every direction. By the time I made sure that Donna and Edna were squared away, things were beginning to run smoothly.

Troy Hicks and Mary Elizabeth Brown were in charge of the sailboats. It was good to have both of them along because sailing was one area in which we did not have a whole lot of volunteers with previous experience. Pete and a few others knew the true ins and outs, but "sailing" people were definitely in the minority. Heaven knew where most of the sailboats would end up. Troy would probably have to go out and help a few back. This would add to his time on the job, but Troy didn't mind.

I mean, Troy didn't mind giving the extra time needed to take care of things on the water. Why once, he unselfishly spent over two hours out on the river in a sailboat. Of course, that time he wasn't trying to help some unlucky camper. He had taken Cayla out for an evening sail, and they *supposedly* got becalmed! That's what they said anyway. It must have been one of those days when there was lots of wind on the shore but none out on the river, I'm sure.

I have to admit that one of the times Pete Smith showed his true colors was at the waterfront. Many a time, I sent him into action to help out an overturned sailboat or canoe. I think he holds the record for the most times stung by nettles, both in one mad dash out and for an entire camp career. One would have thought that the boy would have wised up after a while, but he never once refused to answer the call to rescue. I don't know if it was stupidity, dedication, commitment, loyalty, or care, or perhaps something completely different.

Chuck Paul had finished going over the basics of canoeing, and now several groups were ready to set forth. Most of the canoes were manned, or "womaned," by three people. Each canoe had two volunteers and a camper. With the hearing impaired, it made no difference where they sat, but usually those with the visually impaired had one of the volunteers in the back doing the steering. Still, a few canoes went out with a totally blind person in the back, responding to verbal directions.

A few of the canoes with the youngest campers, ages three and four, had the camper in the middle. Now, in theory, you might think that those canoes with a volunteer in the back were in great shape, but that didn't always work out in practice. Not all of my helpers were that knowledgeable when it came to canoeing. Not many of the canoes kept in a straight line at any time. (I once saw on Facebook the following quote by Pastor Lynn Hardaway: "Remember, when God calls us to a minister, HE has already factored in our own stupidity!")

The first thing I noticed this morning was an exception to the rule. One of the canoes was cutting through the river waters on a straight and true path. When I looked closer, I realized why this was. Howard and Waylon's female counselors had gotten the help Jay Russ. Jay was both a friend and the youth minister at Hampton Baptist Church. He was one of my counselors who could handle his weight, as well as that of the two boys (who were not small), and keep the canoe going in the direction they wanted.

Another favorite activity of the campers was the kayaks. Though a lot easier to turn over, they were fun to take out into the river. Many of the totally blind students would eagerly commandeer a kayak, with their sighted guide paddling alongside. This sometimes put the volunteer in a more stressful situation. In a canoe, you at least have a chance to correct an unbalance. If your camper was in a kayak, often all you could do was watch as they tip over. One thing that really impressed me was that not once did one of the visually impaired overturn and then not want to go back out in a kayak again. They were real troopers.

Another real trooper was Kristine Davis. She once showed the dedication that all our volunteers possessed. Kristine was out with a fellow who could not swim and was a little afraid of the water. Still, he had begged to go out in a kayak, and Kristine was willing to go with him. Naturally, we had followed good camp policy, and the student was wearing a life jacket. Kristine, however, made a mistake in assuming that all would go well. Therefore, she didn't take the time to remove the wristwatch and camera from her person.

Sure enough, about thirty feet away from the end of the dock, her camper capsized. Now, he was wearing his vest, and he was perfectly safe. Nevertheless, Kristine knew how scared he was of the water, and her natural instincts took over. This she did, despite her own fear of crabs. (Hey, all of us have fears, and there are plenty of crabs in that water.) Kristine simply slipped into the water and put her arm around her camper. She then helped him get to his overturned kayak.

By the time I got there in a canoe, all was well. Soon, they were both back in their righted vessels and off to continue their journey. Needless to say, both the watch and camera were no longer in working order.

Like other activities, we had many water skill levels represented. Those who were just learning would spend most of this morning near the dock, getting the hang of things. Possibly, by the end of the session, they would venture out into the river. It was always fun to watch those canoes snake their way across the river and back. A few would spend most of the morning making big circles in the river. It took some of the volunteers a little practice before they got steering down.

A couple of the more experienced groups were headed out for one of two specific destinations: the island or a fossil bank upriver. I quickly scanned the canoes as they started out. My volunteers are great, but they are also human. I knew this was one of the places where their human side might win out, especially on a gorgeously sunny day like today. Sure enough, I caught two offenders, both in the same canoe.

"Lisa Bartlett! Ellen Cykowski! You get those life jackets from under your butts and on your bodies."

With dirty looks directed my way, they complied. I could count, one-hundred percent, on my volunteers to make sure the campers were wearing their jackets. However, in the quest for a perfect tan, they would often try to sneak off, sitting on their own. This was especially true of the strong swimmers, like Ellen and Lisa. They were with Joe Paul, another youngster with unlimited energy.

The canoes were being led by Gail Pearsall. Gail was one of the two staff workers at the Virginia Rehabilitation Center for the Blind who always came along and helped to make this retreat special and safe. Rosetta Robinson was the other, and both went out of their way to bring extra equipment, like crabbing and fishing gear, which were so popular with the kids. Rosetta would generally take care of the fishing, crabbing, and other dockside activities. Being a lifeguard herself, this made Rosetta a valuable person at that site.

The first year we used Piankatank, someone had discovered a section of river bank, about a mile upriver, which was full of prehistoric shells. Some of the clam shells measured over a foot in length. Each year since, Gail would take a group in canoes, making one or more trips to their secret shell grounds. By the end of the retreat, she and many of her students would have enough shells to take care of arts and crafts for the rest of the summer.

Lisa, Ellen, and Joe Paul took off with Edna, Donna, and Grace Marie Mallory right behind. Grace showed up for this one retreat, and then we lost track of her for a while. She was out of Ailor's new church in Richmond, and I continually bugged him to get her back again. She had all the attributes of a great volunteer. She never did make it back on a retreat, but she did end up working in our area and helping out with a lot of other events.

Ailor called one day to let me know Grace was working nearby, and I immediately invited her to come to the Campus Life Burger Bash. She showed up, and we thought she was a high-school student. After getting that straightened out, I introduced her to Steve, Pete, Troy, and Scott. They invited her to church the next morning, and she showed up. Then, for about two months, those four guys followed her around like little puppy dogs. Finally, Ralph got into the act for a while, as did Paul Wygal. Paul was the one who took her away from all of us. Eventually they married and now have two children.

Now, here is the interesting part. That morning, behind Grace and her crew, was another canoe with none other than Paul Wygal and Jeremy. Jeremy was eight years old and stood about four feet tall. He and Paul made quite a contrast. Paul had to reach down just to be able to keep a hand on his head when walking. In this canoe, it was the volunteer who would do most of the work while Jeremy enjoyed the ride. All the while, Paul was following Grace down the river, which is kind of what he has done ever since!

The group canoeing to the island would have the added attraction of a hike. The island was not too large, but there were two nice trails that you could follow. There were camping sites on the island, too, but we never got around to using them. Still the hikes were always a big hit with our campers.

One of the exciting things about life is how often you will meet someone, lose track of them, and then have them show up again when you least expect it. Part of the group paddling out toward the island would later fall into that category. Mike Levy had been one of the first vision-impaired guys we met. He had come on our first one-day outing, and for the next two years, he showed up at every event we sponsored. Mike made sure that I always put him with two girls. He was another one who kept up a running conversation with whoever he was near. Today, Stella Totty and Nancy Hayes were with Mike. These two girls were giving him all the attention he could handle.

Kathy Bowman and Joyce Mayes were in another canoe with Eurika. Eurika and Mike were good friends with the archery duo, Ruth and Belinda. Like the latter, Eurika loved to give me a good-natured hard time. She was also one of the campers who went out of her way to make sure that all the volunteers were having a good time and that life was treating them well. All four were committed Christians, who looked well beyond their own handicaps. About two years later, I would lose track of these four for over a decade.

Then, sometime in the 1990s, I was asked to talk to a blind support group, which met at the local library. I had not met Polly, the person who called to set things up, and I did not know if I would know any of the others. Imagine my surprise when I walked in and saw Eurika, Ruth, Belinda, and Mike. Since that time, we have renewed our friendship with fishing trips and retreat days and other events.

Dee Dee Hartless and Joyce Brown

Above: Pete to the rescue. There were wall-to-wall stinging nettles in the river that day.
Below: Howard and Waylon head in to shore with Jay Russ.

Left: Scott Millar and a camper enjoy the day.

25
On the Waterfront

*A*fter seeing the canoes off, I moved on toward the pier, where Rosetta was in charge of the fishing and crabbing. When the pool was not open, most of the younger kids gravitated here. As I walked out onto the pier, I was passed by a group coming the other way. Tammi, who I picked up on the way to camp, and her friend Susan were signing away to Josie and three younger volunteers: Tami Smith, Karen Watts, and Susan Williams. I started to ask them where they were going, and then decided I probably didn't want to know. Ignorance is bliss.

The dock was also where some of the group would come out to sun themselves. Here, they could legally leave life jackets off and relax. I found Lloyd, Elise, and Shannon, but they were not relaxing. In fact, they seemed to be in deep conversation. I tried to follow what was being signed, but I was soon lost. Their conversation was complicated. Lloyd could sign to the girls in a normal way, but since he was visually and hearing impaired, they had to sign in his hand for him to understand.

Surprisingly, they kept up this serious interchange the whole time I was on the dock. The only time this changed was when one of the volunteers carried a crab over to Elise, so she could "show it" to Lloyd. She held the claws while Shannon signed what he was about to take hold of. Then Elise placed his hands on the wriggling creature.

This was Lloyd's second year with us. He was a cheerful young man in his early twenties. He had been born deaf and had started to go blind during his early teens. He had a little bit of speech and knew sign language. Now he was both deaf and totally blind.

Elise will kill me for telling this story, but I can't resist. It always seemed like something funny was happening to Elise. The prior year, Lloyd showed us that being blind and deaf did not affect his normal male feelings. Elise had been communicating with Lloyd, and he was teaching her some new signs. As I said earlier, with a deaf and blind individual, you have to either sign in their hands or use their hands to make the sign. They had come to the word *how*, which is signed by putting your hands to your chest and then pulling them out with the palms up. Without thinking, in learning to sign *how*, Elise had taken Lloyd's hands and put them to her chest. After they had gone over the signs for a few more words, Elise decided that Lloyd might like to go to another activity.

She asked, "Lloyd, what do you want to do next?"

Lloyd spoke some of the clearest words I had heard him pronounce when he answered, "Let's sign *how* again!"

Elise laughed and told him that they were going canoeing!

Lloyd was always willing to try something new. He was a young man with a lot going against him. Not only was he both deaf and blind, but he had several diseases, including diabetes. Gail had shared with me at the beginning of this retreat that the doctors did not give him long to live. Still, he faced life with a smile and a positive attitude. He really impressed me with his desire to do all that he could in life.

I was about to become even more impressed. Shannon put the crab back in the basket and took Lloyd's hand to "talk" some more. Elise came over to where Rosetta and I were standing. She had a plan and wanted our permission to carry it out.

～

As Elise was finishing the explanation of her scheme, Cherie Bradley and Lori Blankenship were walking past some beached canoes on their way to the pier. Cherie was about to give a very graphic demonstration of the old phrase, "a split second." She was one of those special people who soon forgot that you have a handicap. To Cherie, you were a person, and that was all that really mattered.

A few minutes earlier, she had shown just how completely most of us got caught up with this group of friends. Nathan had been sitting in a chair outside the girls' bathroom, waiting for Cherie and Lori to change into bathing suits. Cherie was the first to come out, and when she did, she saw Nathan sitting with his back to the bathhouse. She got a big smile on her face and quietly walked up behind Nathan. She slowly reached her arms around and placed her hands over his eyes.

"Guess who!"

Even as she said the words, Cherie realized what she had done. Her face turned beet red. Nathan laughed and said without missing a beat, "Cherie, you ain't a bit sneaky. I could hear you coming a mile away!"

Cherie smiled at her sightless friend, gave him a big hug, and said, "Let's go, pal."

Lori joined them at that moment, and the three walked hand in hand down the path to the river. It was a beautiful day, and Cherie was enjoying it to the fullest. Always full of energy, she could not be content with walking down the pier this morning. She asked Lori to lead Nathan to the end of the dock while she followed with some acrobatics. Cherie waited for them to get well ahead, and then she gave in to her natural exuberance. She began to make her way out onto the pier doing a series of cartwheels.

Cherie was giving a pretty good exhibition, except for one small mistake, which had escaped her notice. Every time she came down, both feet ended up nearer and nearer the side of the pier. Finally, the inevitable happened. On her next landing, she came to a stop with both heels off the edge of the pier. For a second, much longer than a split second, she tottered on the edge. As she lost her balance, she made a small jump backward to clear the pier.

Up to this point, Cherie remained calm, despite the fact that she was standing in two feet of water and who knew how much mud. I started to call out a warning, but Nathan beat me to it. Lori had been giving him a "landing by landing" description of the scene, and when she told him that Cherie had jumped off the pier, Nathan knew the danger. He had been at camp before and was well acquainted with the ins and outs of the Piankatank River.

Even over the sound of the splash he was yelling, "Cherie! Be careful. There are water moccasins around the pier!"

I was there. I saw this with my own eyes. This is a firsthand account. When Nathan said the words *water moccasins*, Cherie was still standing with both feet flat in the water. Before he got the word *pier* out of his mouth, she was standing back up on the pier. Cherie had her areas of athletic ability, but I would never have thought the high jump was one of them. She managed a three-and-one-half-foot standing high jump off a muddy riverbed.

I decided to get out of there before I saw something that would really make me think we were all in big trouble. On these retreats, we really did learn to trust in Jesus and the God-given ability of our friends to overcome any problems, even those we brought upon ourselves. I knew this was always true, but I still tended to worry too much about these events. One of my own hang-ups is that, if I am in charge of something, I am always trying to convince myself that something out of the ordinary won't happen. It hardly ever did, but that didn't keep me from worrying about it.

The final irony was that, when something did crop up, we always found a way to deal with it. It was true that all of us, most certainly myself, were human, and we did our fair share of stupid stunts. However, I can say that no one on these retreats ever did anything stupid on purpose or out of disregard. If we had any shortcomings, they came out of our enjoying life and being with each other. Still, I must admit, if I ever had any questions about God's guiding hand, they were dispelled by these retreats. He really seemed to keep a watch over us. **His love is definitely not blind!**

We certainly tried to do the same things on these retreats that you would do on any youth retreat. Some of our events were a little tricky to pull off, and sometimes it was easy to worry a little. However, things always went well, and usually by the end of the day, we could even think back on the mistakes with a smile.

Before this morning was over, Chuck and Pete would have to take a canoe out to where one of the sailboats had been swamped. It was important to get to them quickly because the Piankatank River had wall-to-wall stinging nettles. One year, Pete paid the ultimate price by swimming through a mass of stinging nettles to get to an overturned canoe, which held a couple of our youngest campers. It turned out that everyone was fine, but Pete was taking no chances. He moved gingerly for the rest of the weekend, but his actions typified our general attitude.

There was one major mistake this morning that could have been bad, but even that one turned out fine. Two of my counselors came in with a totally blind guy in the back. Now, Lloyd Brown's and Darrin Lawing's intentions were noble. Their camper still had his shoes on, and they wanted to be sure his feet stayed dry. The problem was that the camper was standing up, unsupported in the canoe, when both guys grabbed the rope tied off in the front and began to tug. Each thought the other was with their guy. Their camper did a great imitation of a high-wire walker as he struggled, successfully, to keep his balance. I was amazed how well he did.

We also got the whole episode on film. It was a mistake they will never forget. We won't let them!

Above left: Denise Harris on our first overnighter

Above right: Cherie Bradley

Left: Katherine Michillie

Above left: Vawnetta Johnson and Carol Gwaltney, both of whom worked for me as summer missionaries (Smishies) *Above right:* Brooke Puckett with Carol Gwaltney
Below: Marianne Mahone, sighted guide

26
Lynne

Over the years, we got to know many vision- and hearing-impaired adults. Some, like Carol Gwaltney, we came to know as close friends. Carol was a member of one of our churches. She met Steve Skinner, and he invited her to come on one of our retreats. Then, as usual, he asked if that was OK with me. As usual, it was fine.

Carol was in her late thirties, living at home with her mom. She loved the retreat, and we all enjoyed getting to know her. She kept going with us, and after a few years, I asked her if she would work with us on the Smishy team. To be honest that might also have been Skinner's idea. She was thrilled.

Carol was a great help at the Vacation Bible Schools because she was so talented musically. She was always willing to lead in singing songs. Another of her good qualities was that she did not mind talking to children about her limitations and explaining how they should act as a sighted guide. She added a lot to any trip she went on.

Carol was also adept at helping with crafts. She excelled at one particular craft, which has cost us a lot of dollars over the years. She made yarn-covered coat hangers, which are great for decorations or for hanging items on. I have about twenty of them, and most of the Smishies who have worked for me during those years have at least two or three. In this one area, she was very capitalistic. She gave me my first one as a present, but I had to pay for all the rest. The same was true for all my Smishies.

One of the best friendships that developed over the years was that of Carol and Vawnetta Johnson. Vawnetta worked as both a volunteer and as a Smishy, doing a superb job at each. Theirs was another example of a friendship that went beyond the time spent in ministry.

Others we have met and walked with for only a short period of time. Like each of us, they have their own story. Some of these stories would tug at your heart. The group coming from Richmond each year tended to be an older lot; thus, they had been through a lot more of life and it wasn't always easy.

As I was leaving Cherie Bradley to dry off her feet, I glanced back and saw Lynne Everhart and her vision-impaired friend from the rehab center sitting on the end of the dock. Lynne was one of my oldest-running "teen" friends. I had known her since she was six. Phil and Lucille Everhart's home had been one of my own drop-in places over the years, along with the Ailors'. Lynne had helped out with the early probation retreats we did shortly after I started my ministry with the PBA.

From there, she and her dog Blue had gone on to help me with our retreats for foster kids, as well as a number of other ministries, including this camp. Easy-going and agreeable, Lynne was one of those people you just liked being with. She had a great outlook on life and liked to be with people.

Lynne, along with her brother Phil and Jimmy Ailor, were possibly three of the first younger teens, which I considered actual friends. While in junior high, she wrote the following, which her mother now displays in her front hall:

> *This is not primarily the place*
> *where we have to be,*
> *it is the place we are.*
>
> *This is not our prison but our*
> *home. It is the road we must*
> *walk and walking of it is called life.*
>
> *Because we will walk it only once, then*
> *how important is it that we walk it*
> *with some purpose we can call our own.*

Lynne's companion on this retreat, Helena, made her first big impression on us the night before at the talent show. She kind of stole the show. We were winding down and had only one act left, that being done by two of Jimmy Ailor's youth. Renee Barnes and Cole Bailey were performing a Johnny Carson routine, and as such, they invited someone from the audience to come up.

Helena volunteered, and they brought her to the front, expecting to have to draw out a few comments from her. Then, they planned to let her sit down while they continued. It was a mistake, as far as their act was concerned, but a great moment for the rest of us. She answered the first question and proceeded to take over. In fact, within two minutes, Renee and Cole, graciously and without offense, faded into the background and let Helena have center stage.

She kept it up for a half hour, giving a running monologue, which included humorous jabs at me, what it's like being blind, camp volunteers, other campers, and life in general. She had a natural talent, and we were sorry when it was all over. Her wit was sharp, but there was a part of her that was even sharper. She loved to speak in front of any group about her own Christian testimony. For the next two years, Helena would call from time to time and tell me about speaking engagements, most of which centered around the topics of being blind and being a daughter of God.

At this moment, she and Lynne were sitting at the end of the dock with fishing poles in their hands; however, fishing was the last thing on their minds. Listening to Helena joke could make you think she did not have an enemy or a care in the world, other than her vision problems. But it seemed she did have one enemy out there somewhere in the world—her husband.

Helena was an abused wife, who on more than one occasion had been beaten near to death. In fact, Helena was not her real name. She was from another state but had come to the Richmond rehab center because, she hoped, her husband would not know where she was. Helena has long since moved on, but many of us will never forget her.

Left: Susie Hyatt

Below: Denise Harris and Lynne Ever-hart

27
Peggy & Susie

Our friends faced the same good and bad life situations, which can hit all of us from time to time. However, in Helena's case, one thing was certain. She was determined to continue to leave a good mark on the people she met along the way. We could all learn from that kind of determination. Each of us encounter mountains in our paths, and certainly many of my own volunteers had tall mountains that they were in the midst of climbing. The only real difference I could see was that the campers had one additional peak to scale.

Jimmy Ailor and a couple of the volunteers had gotten to know another totally blind girl named Peggy. Also from the rehabilitation center, she was a quiet and serious young lady. They were spending this morning at the pavilion just talking. She, like Helena, had a greater need to talk than to engage in activities. Jimmy later related the story she told to them.

Peggy had grown up in a poor section of her city. Her mother, who had been deserted by her husband when Peggy was five, had worked long hours at minimum wages to try and make ends meet. There was little or no money left for anything else. The one thing Peggy had been able to hold onto was her health. Then, sometime around her sixteenth birthday, she began to experience migraine headaches. Peggy's mom could not afford to take her to a private doctor, but when she progressed to periods of dizziness and blurred vision, she took her to the health department.

Because no physical cause could be found, and taking into account her past good health, Peggy's condition was diagnosed as mental. It seemed to make sense, given her family background. The attending physician recommended psychiatric help. The recommendation was of course, academic. There was no psychiatrist working with the health department. If her mom could not afford a private medical doctor, she certainly could not pay to take Peggy to a private psychiatrist.

Within six months, Peggy had gone completely blind. In the meantime, her mom had been put in touch with the state psychiatric hospital. After losing her vision, Peggy was admitted and treated for a psychosomatic disorder, with no apparent success.

Finally, she was given a complete physical examination. It was then that they discovered that Peggy had a brain tumor. It was causing her blindness, and to make matters worse, it was inoperable. She was given four to five years to live, and then sent home, still blind. Despite that knowledge, Peggy had regained her high spirits. She was no longer locked up in an institution, and now at least she knew what she was battling.

～

Although not near as tragic, this part of Peggy's story reminded me of what Mrs. Riddle went through with Shannon. Shortly after Shannon was born, she knew something was not right. Her daughter was slow in developing speech, did not seem to listen, and missed normal audio cues. She took Shannon to a series of army hospital doctors but was always given the same answer. Nothing was really wrong. Her daughter was probably just slow in developing.

Finally, on one visit, she got fed up and demanded to see the chief doctor. He came into the examining room and listened to what Mrs. Riddle had to say. The doctor then performed a very simple test. He walked behind the infant and loudly clapped his hands next to each ear. When Shannon failed to respond to either clap, the doctor turned and said that Shannon was deaf!

Most of our friends were an inspiration. In the group of hearing impaired on this retreat, none typified this more than Shannon Riddle. She had been born deaf but was fully integrated into a hearing world. Her parents made sure of that. They loved her and looked out for her, but they did not shield her from the world in which she had to live. They allowed her to fall down, get up, and start over again, both physically and emotionally. She attended one of the local public high schools and would soon become one of my volunteers and Smishies. She was typical of my helpers in that she was very intelligent and could make good grades, when she put her mind to it. Alas, she was another one that did not always put her mind to her studies.

Shannon would not let you exclude her. If someone did not know sign language, and she wanted to be a part of what they were doing, she would include herself. Then she would start teaching them sign language. Shannon was also a gifted athlete. She played softball and flag football for me over the years. In addition, she was an excellent snow skier and a decent water-skier. She was comfortable in the water and passed my YMCA lifeguarding course. She would later accompany a group of us to Florida on snorkeling trips.

Shannon was not the most patient person in the world when it came to waiting for an activity to start. However, in teaching others sign language, she had an abundance of patience. She used to help me with games and teaching sign in a church camp for younger girls. Each day of the camp, Shannon would have to answer the same questions over and over again, as different girls came to her and signed the only sentences they knew:

"How old are you?"

"How are you doing?"

"Do you like camp?"

"Do you remember my name?"

Shannon was also patient with us on Friday nights. For several years, we would meet at her house, where Mrs. Riddle taught us more sign language. We spent as much time laughing on those evenings as we did learning our lessons.

The Sisters Paschal would get into sisterly arguments at times. If they occurred on Friday nights, they would slow their comments down to the point where they could try and sign what they were yelling at each other. It was terrific slow-motion comedy. (Especially the night they didn't know the real sign for the word *but*. Each time the word *but* came up in their argument, they would, with slow and pointed movements, point to their butts.)

Susie Hyatt was Jimmy Ailor's companion volunteer that day as they listened to Peggy's story. Later that night, when I saw the three of them sitting at the campfire together, it seemed like Peggy was at peace with the world. None of us knew it, but within a decade, not only Peggy but also Susie would pass on from this world to a far better place—a place of light and vision and freedom from pain. But before that time came, each would continue to make a real contribution to the world around them.

It should not be assumed that every camper had a sad story, although quite a few of them did. It was certainly a group of people who had to deal with their specific limitations, but of course, all of us have things in life with which we have to contend.

Polly (who never came on the camps but did join us in several boat charter fishing trips) had a great job at the library; Mike Levy, Belinda, Eurika, and Ruth were in love with life; Big Al and the rest of the "Thunderbird Five" were among some of the best wrestlers in the state. A couple of them ranked in the top ten. The rehabilitation center had sent us barbers and college students, singers and songwriters, basketball stars and librarians, among many others. Because we specifically asked for any who could not afford the events or had special needs, we tended to get somewhat of an atypical group, but that was fine. We enjoyed meeting every single camper who ever came on any of the retreats.

The rest of Saturday morning was spent in continuing the activities. Most of them slowed down when we finally opened the pool. By lunch time, almost everyone would have finally gravitated there. After lunch, we had the softball game. These were usually pretty competitive. We had the beeping softball (larger than a traditional softball and which emitted a loud beep each second), but we still found that the best way for us to play was using "Siamese Softball." Josie O'Kane's dad got his retirement group to get us the ball.

The hearing-impaired kids would play regular softball. But we used a tee-ball stand for the visually impaired. As soon as the ball was hit, they would reach out for their counselor's hand, and the two would run the bases together. Defensive players were also linked hand in hand. The sighted guide could run with their camper to the ball and then tell them where it was. The camper had to pick the ball up and make any play. Other than that, we played regular softball rules.

These games usually lasted an hour or two and seemed to be well enjoyed. When this particular game was over, I called everyone over to the pavilion and told them that we had a special event coming up.

Above: Kathy Smith with the beeping softball

Left: Ellen Hamlett

Left: Bill Sinclair and Kevin Ely, 1977 camp

Above: Softball, with Celeste running and Jim George in the background

28
Lloyd Takes a Drive

*T*he activity highlight of the retreat was about to take place, with Elise and Lloyd taking center stage. Shannon had helped with the planning, but everything now fell on the shoulders of the other two. I gave Elise the high sign to proceed with her special project. This was to be the fulfillment of Lloyd's secret dream. I knew everyone would want to be a part of this, and so I assembled us all together to ring the big field. Elise went to get her car.

In talking with Lloyd on Friday night, Elise had discovered that his secret dream was to drive an automobile. During his sighted years, Lloyd had looked forward to when he could get his license. As his vision faded, driving became one of life's privileges that would be denied. Still, at least once in his lifetime, Lloyd wanted to be behind the wheel of a moving car.

Using the slow and tedious method of signing into his hands, Elise explained that she would be glad to teach him to drive a car. She would let him do so here at camp. For Lloyd, this event became the main focus of this year's retreat. He knew sign and could even speak a little. Normally, this would have meant that half the communication battle was won. However, when Elise explained just how they would work this out, Lloyd became excited and began to sign at a much faster pace than usual. Elise tried to get him to slow down, but every time they got into it, he would invariably speed up, thus losing her for a few seconds.

(Nowadays, two of the first words I teach in sign class are (1) *slow*—right hand facing down with fingers on the back of the left hand, then run the fingers up past the wrist—and (2) *again*—with the left hand open and facing up, put the tips of the right hand fingers into the open palm. I explain, truthfully, that these will be two of their most used words initially.)

Elise came up with a simple but ingenious solution to this problem. It involved a three-sided conversation. Lloyd would answer Elise's instructions with flying hands and a few words. If needed, Shannon would then slowly sign the same answer to Elise. It had taken all morning to make sure Lloyd knew what would happen and how, but by lunch, they had a "pat" method of driving signals down pat: A pat on either shoulder told him which way to turn the wheel. The back of the neck became a speed indicator, and the top of Lloyd's head was used to indicate when and how long to brake. Elise had decided to give Lloyd the full measure of driving pleasure, and she was going to let him use her car. (Well, you didn't think I was going to let them use mine, did you?) It had a standard transmission. Pats on the knee were shift instructions.

Just like that, Lloyd was sitting in the driver's seat. Elise had driven it up close to the pavilion, with the front facing toward the swimming pool in the distance. She got into the passenger side and signed to Lloyd that she was ready when he was. The flagpole was some ten feet away, standing to the right of the car. I figured if he didn't hit that and if he didn't make a dive into the swimming pool at the other end of the field, he just might come out of this thing all right. Elise might come out of it with a still drivable car, and I might still have a job. I will admit it—I was a teeny bit nervous, but I wasn't about to put a stop to it. To be honest, I was fascinated by the whole idea. Still, part of my mind was wondering, *Just how do you get a car out of a swimming pool?*

Volunteers were giving the other vision-impaired students a turn-by-turn description. I watched as the car started with a series of jerks. (Before Craig says it, I know the biggest jerk was not in the car!) It never stalled, however, and soon you could hear Lloyd shifting gears and picking up speed as he headed toward the swimming pool.

"Hey," I said to no one in particular, "isn't this supposed to be a very slow and leisurely drive around the field? Isn't he going a little fast?" I turned to ask Ailor if he didn't think the same thing, but Ailor was too intent on watching to pay any attention to me.

Later, Elise told me what transpired during the drive. What I didn't know was that Elise was determined to let Lloyd have the drive of his life, and to heck with whatever heart attacks the camp director might have. She refused to pat Lloyd's head (slow down/stop) as the swimming pool fence began to fill the windshield. (At least, it seemed that way to Elise's eyes. This was one time when ignorance was bliss. Lloyd was simply following Elise's directions and enjoying the thrill of the ride. *What swimming pool?*)

At the last possible instant, she gave him a pat on the shoulder, indicating a right turn. Elise knew this was the most critical moment of the entire activity. She had allowed him to go a little faster than originally intended, and it was crucial he made a correct turn at this point. If Lloyd got confused at this moment, everyone was in for a long afternoon. Lloyd knew what to do. It was just that he took his time in doing it. Finally, when it seemed that the car would take the plunge, Lloyd made as smart a right turn as you could ask.

Elise kept him turning right while slowly applying the brakes. Then they came back up the field. In a surprisingly short period of time, old Lloyd was driving like a pro. He was turning all sorts of ways and giving the gas every time he got the proper tap. It was soon apparent that "giving it the gas" was his favorite tap.

I'm not sure who showed the greatest amount of faith that day, Elise or Lloyd. (Or perhaps Gail and Rosetta for allowing this to take place!) It was certainly a graphic object lesson in believing in the abilities of a friend. If not for her faith in Jesus, I know Elise would not have been in that car. I kind of think the same was true for Lloyd. On the other hand, they had to have faith in each other also. Lloyd had to believe that Elise would not lead him off the straight "path," and Elise put her faith in Lloyd, believing that he would respond in the manner they had discussed. The reality of this situation is that they could easily have ended up in the swimming pool. They didn't because each approached the event in a responsible manner, showing the necessary faith in each other and in the Lord.

Just how important was that half hour car ride in the scheme of Lloyd's life? I can't answer that question. What I do know is that, when they finished, Lloyd had a grin the size of the Grand Canyon on his face. That half hour became Lloyd's chief topic of conversation for the rest of the retreat. We never saw Lloyd again after that weekend was over. His health continued to go downhill over the winter, and he was not able to make the retreat the next summer. Shortly after that retreat, Gail and Rosetta let us know that Lloyd had passed away. The good news is that now Lloyd can see, and not through a mirror dimly. He has perfect vision in a perfect place.

Elise eventually married John Hogge, one of the midnight raiders we had been chasing so few hours before. She later graduated from nursing school and worked for a while in the ICU unit. John went to work at the shipyard. Shannon is still in the general area; Tammy George hears from her occasionally. Life goes on.

Above and left:
Elise, Lloyd, and
Shannon discuss
car-driving lessons.

29
Steve's Motorcycle Adventure

*I*n the last chapter, I mentioned the fact that Lloyd was driving like a pro. His driving was a lot safer than Pete Smith's or Steve Burnette's. A few years later, they had an interesting experience before our retreat.

To fully explain what is to follow, I need to answer a question that Craig Waddell once asked. He asked if I spent much time before the retreats worrying about the possibility of a lot of helpers not being able to make it at the last minute, leaving us short-handed. I answered, honestly, that I didn't, but I often worried about the possibility of a lot of campers not making it, which would mean I had many more volunteer helpers than needed. The problem—and I assure you that it *would* have been a problem—was that, as long as they had "responsibilities," my volunteers were the most attentive and on-task people you could ask for.

However, I also knew that if I had a lot of helpers who didn't need to be looking after campers or leading events, their natural mischievous nature could lead to even more problems than I did naturally encounter. We never had too much help, but one time only, we were far below what I would have liked (one counselor for each hearing-impaired camper, two for each vision-impaired camper, and enough to lead at each event happening at the time). That one exception leads me to the story of Steve and Pete.

It was a year when a lot of my veteran counselors were not able to make it. We had a smaller, though proficient, staff going, but I could ill afford to lose any of them. Two of my best guys were Pete and Steve. My girls' softball team played the night before, and both of the guys were there. After the game, I left for home and told the Group I would see them in the morning. As I was leaving, another friend rode up on a motorcycle. I didn't pay that much attention.

About 2 AM my phone rang. It was Pete. He sounded tired and out of breath. I asked him why he was so out of breath. He told me he had just jogged two miles down the interstate with a can of gas. I told Pete I was sorry, but as he had already accomplished this, why had he called me? Did his car not start, and he needed a lift? Pete told me that the car was now running. That was the good news.

Immediately, I was wide awake. I didn't have to ask for the bad news. Pete went on to say he and Steve had been on the way home from the hospital at Fort Eustis, and he had not paid attention to his gas gauge. They had run out of gas on the interstate while returning home. Pete said the highlight of the night had come as he was jogging down the interstate, heading for the nearest exit. He had come upon a brightly lit section of road, where a gang of highway department workers were doing some repairs. Pete said he waved to this amazed crew working away in the night. He kind of felt like the "Midnight Jogger." On the way back, Pete had to listen to a few special comments from the workers.

I was about to prod Pete to get back to the hospital bit, when he went on to explain the initial problem. Steve had been playing around with the motorcycle at the ballfield parking lot, thinking himself a stunt rider. The main stunt of the night was when he laid the bike down on the pavement trying to make a turn. The skin on his back had not fared too well. Thus the midnight trip to the hospital.

Pete said that he figured he would get home about 5 AM. He was still going on the retreat, but he didn't know how effective he would be in the morning. Steve, of course, was out of commission! Pete said that Steve was not seriously hurt and was going to be OK.

"Who cares!" I shouted over the phone.

I was a bit upset. OK, I was more than a bit upset at my good friend Steve Burnette. (I am not really proud of my feelings at that moment, but because I expressed them to Pete, I might as well own up to them here.) Steve was in pain, but all I could think was, *Oh, great. We are hurting for counselors as it is, and now I've lost two of my best.* (At least I held Steve in high regard, right?) I told Pete that I hoped Steve was in pain! (I mean, what are friends for if not to think of each other in times of need.)

132

To be honest, I probably hit an all-time low in both my reliance on the Lord and my caring for friends. While on the phone that night, I was convinced that the retreat would be a disaster; people would probably get killed, and who knew what other bad things would happen.

The next day, the Lord let me know once again that He and He alone was in charge of the results of anything we do for Him. Pete went on the retreat. He slept in the infirmary till noon, but then he was his old self. The counselors—and indeed we were short-handed—did great, and the retreat went fine. By ten the next morning, I was feeling appropriately foolish and was fervently praying that Steve was out of pain and getting better. Most importantly, Steve forgave me! (At least I think he did, and it is too late to worry about that now!)

Barbara Vinson

Above: More initiative events (Corinne Powell and Sarah Panganeban are on the end.)
Right: Brendan Lawson shows how it's done.
Below left: Vision-impaired camper, Travis, earned a repelling certificate at the camp.
Below right: Camper learns to repel.

30
We Are All in This Together

One of our goals on any of the events we sponsored for special groups was to give them a chance to experience the same things that most of us had fun doing. Often back home, we would be in the middle of an enjoyable afternoon when someone would say, "Hey, we should check with the school or the rehab center and see if they would like to try this with their trainees."

That is exactly how the snow-skiing trips started. Josie Paul literally turned to Chuck, Bob Moore, and me while standing at the top of a ski lift and said, "Hey, we should try this with the Group." And we did.

The next really unusual event we did at camp came several years later with a new group of counselors. The state Baptist association added a repelling tower to the camp's activities. This was the same year that Craig Waddell made his return to Camp Piankatank with a group of Austrian and Romanian youth from his church in Linz, Austria. I also had my two Latvian girls working with me that summer. Anyway, with all the extra help available, we ran a week-long camp instead of a three-day retreat. This meant that one of the regular summer week camps for church youth was being run at Piankatank at the same time.

It was a great experience, both for our campers and for the youth who were at Piankatank. We got most of our special campers to at least try the sloping wall. Aaron Whittington and Ralf Schlitcher (from Austria) worked with a young man named Travis. Travis, who was totally blind, tried every activity that the camp offered. He was the one person from our gang who repelled the taller wall.

Craig's group of Austrians and Romanians arrived in D.C. on a Friday afternoon, and we spent the weekend with Ailor and other families from his church in Northern Virginia. Steve Burnette and I took the two Latvian girls (Ieva and Liga) and drove the PBA vans to meet the plane. (That trip to D.C. is a story in itself.) Returning to Hampton, we stopped off at the rehab center, where Rosetta gave us a tour and some training for the upcoming week.

At the end of the camp week, each of the campers (ours and the other youth) received certificates for the skills they had mastered. Every one of our group got at least one. Travis, however, was by far the best camper of the week. Working with Ralf and Aaron, he collected several certificates and was loved and respected by all the regular camp staff. Keith Stainker, the camp director, did a great job of integrating the two groups so that all of us got the most from the week.

Not only was a climbing wall added, but also an initiative called the Spider Web. This is a giant web made of sting, with a number of different-sized holes. You have to pass your team through the web, using each hole only once, and not touching the sides of the spider web. It's a lot of fun, and while we hit the sides of the web many times (which results in "death" in the usual scenario for this initiative), we did get the entire team through the web. We decided that we had plenty of anti-venom.

"Sittin' on the Dock of the Bay": Jeff Lacky, camper, Sarah Pangannebian, Jamie Napier, camper, Laura Davis, and Heather Parker (seated); Shirley Gay, Jeremy Young, Brooke Puckett, and Carol Gwaltney

31

The Pigeons

*O*ften, it seemed that our events alternated between the poignant and the humorous. Steve Skinner provided some unintentional light humor just before dinner. Steve, who is now a veterinarian, always loved being around animals, be it underwater or on land. On our retreats, we could count on Steve to come upon a turtle, a lizard, or some other type of animal. We would then call a time out to whatever was going on and have an impromptu nature study. This would give all of us a chance to see and feel one of the many small living creatures roaming the camp.

This year, Steve had brought several of his pets from home. The campers were in for a special treat. This day's nature study would not be impromptu. It was a planned event, which included not only nature, but any item that some of the campers had perhaps not experienced before.

We got the idea from the Smithsonian's Discovery Room. Naturally, we copied the idea. We even copied the name.

(A few years back, I attended a seminar with Harald Aadahl, Wes Garrett, Ben Sandford, Tommy Rowe, and Jay Russ. In between playing Frisbee golf, hearts, real golf, and eating ribs, we did go to several of the seminars. At one, we were told that the four keys to being creative with any group are as follows: see what works for other people and then copy, copy, copy, and finally copy!)

Starting this year, we had a Discovery period, where counselors could bring anything they thought might be of interest to the campers. In future years, this would include such items as coral, musical instruments, a metal detector, animal skins, golf clubs, fish bones, and even a human skull (courtesy of Bob Moore, who found it while digging in a river bank the year before).

This year highlighted Skinner and some of his pets. One of them he was saving for a special time later. (He could wait forever to show Alice, as far as I was concerned!) For the opening session, he proudly brought out three homing pigeons. Over the years, I have found our campers to be among the best students you could have. I watched a camp full of youth and adults hang onto every word Steve spoke. First, he passed the birds around so that everyone could know how they felt in their hands. In addition to "feeling," the hearing impaired got a close-up view of the birds.

Steve went on to tell about the care and feeding of pigeons. Finally, he shared about the training and racing of these intelligent creatures. Then came the part all the campers had been waiting for. Even I began to get a little more excited when Steve explained their homing abilities. He told us that he had taken the three out of their cage at home yesterday morning. In spite of the fifty-mile drive and overnight accommodations in a strange environment, they would all three be back at his home when he got there tomorrow. We would get to see them begin their flight home. At least that was what Steve Skinner told us.

Everyone stood up when Steve was ready to release the birds. He knew that many young people often expected immediate results. Thinking ahead (now why can't I ever do that?), he told us that it might take a few minutes for the pigeons to get their bearings. During that time, they would most likely fly in circles around the camp.

He looked right at Jimmy and Craig and said, "So no comments if they don't head right off. Everything will work out fine."

Keeping in mind the layout of the camp, Steve went on to say that when they did depart, we should look for them to fly over the swimming pool and away from camp in that direction.

By now, everyone had been given a chance to hold one of the birds. Steve picked three of the vision-impaired youngsters to be the ones to let them go. Now those three were holding them with soft but firm fingers. Steve told them to hold their arms straight out and, on his command, let them loose. Three sets of arms extended outward and upward.

"Now!" shouted Steve, and the three birds lifted from the human hands. They rose quickly and headed right for the swimming pool. A few claps of applause were muffled when they swung to the right, flew back toward us along the tree line, and then circled behind us, coming back into view over the cafeteria.

Steve had that smug look of one who knew exactly what would happen. He didn't even look perplexed when they repeated the exact maneuver. However, he did show a little bit of surprise at what happened next. Their third circle was a tight one right over the cafeteria. Then they simply settled down on the ridge cap of the roof.

I can use the term *ridge cap* because I am a roofer now. I mean, I have done shingling for four days, and I know roofs. I'm just not sure how to spell the word!

I needed to re-shingle my house, and Pete and Steve convinced me that we could do it. I said I wasn't going near the top-story roof, but they said no problem. We got Harald Aadahl, Scott Scheepers, John Whitsel, and Chuck and Josie and their boys to help out. I actually did a little more than I planned and even got up on the top roof. Of course, I never got closer than three feet to any of the edges, so my help was limited, but what the heck. I don't want to rub in the fact that Steve Burnette had to sit out one day because his back was giving him trouble.

All in all, it was a great job. I have to give Pete credit as the only one besides me who spent all four days on the roof, and he would even go near the edges. The final compliment came from my neighbor a few houses down. She said she had never seen and heard any group of people having so much fun roofing a house.

Since first writing this, I am proud to say that, thanks to Harald, I am now the veteran of four roof jobs done during Work Camps, and I can now get closer to the edges.

Steve told the waiting assembly that this was indeed a little unusual, but not completely unexpected. Pigeons, like other animals and people, were sometimes independently minded. They had only decided to take a rest before heading home. Soon, they would be on their way. Turned out, they were evidently not in any hurry to get home. (Or perhaps they were really tired!) They were still sitting on the roof when we went in for dinner, and they were there to greet us when we came back out.

Someone suggested to Steve that perhaps all the shouting the night before had kept them awake. Or perhaps it was simply the result of having lost the road map. It wasn't until the next morning that we saw they had finally flown the coop. To this day, Steve swears they were waiting for him when he got home. I don't know. Perhaps they were, but I'll tell you what I think. Based on their earlier actions, which were an obvious attempt to humiliate their owner, I think those pigeons were a lot like my volunteers. I believe they waited till about 2 AM the next morning and then arrived with as much commotion as they could make.

Above: Kathy, Nathan, and Steve in *MissionsUSA*

Left: Holly Thompson during our Discovery Time

Opposite: Ellen Cykowski helps a camper look for pennies in the sawdust.

Above: Camp Piankatank 1978 (missing the rehab center participants, who had already left)

Below: Goodbye till next year (Lisa Bartlett and Sharon Halsey front right)

32
Ailor: Telling It Like It Is

$\mathscr{S}$teve's pigeons provided one of the highlights of comic relief for the
retreat, and Lloyd's driving adventure provided the most unusual activity of
the weekend. However, the inspirational culmination of this particular retreat
came on Saturday night, when Jim Ailor did the creative worship service. It
was simply the most moving outdoor service I have ever attended.

It was at the campfire at the close of the evening. The previous night,
there had been stories and fun and games. (More fun and games for some than
others.) On this night, we started with s'mores and soft drinks, and after a few
choruses lead by Sinclair, Jim Ailor stood up beside the fire.

We had decided to make this our main worship service and have a shorter
devotional time on Sunday morning. Jim's message, for me at least, was a real
mountaintop experience. He expressed what life is all about. It was even more
special because of the people sitting around me, both campers and volunteers.
Some of my best friends and I were listening to a message that spoke directly
to the fears and obstacles and joys that come with living.

The message was simple, although, as usual, Jim's method of presen-
tation was a little more involved. He began by passing out several items we
would be using to accentuate his points. Pieces of paper and a bag of ten-pen-
ny nails were passed from row to row, while Jim reached behind a nearby tree
and brought out a large wooden cross and two hammers. He laid them next to
the fire and then for the moment ignored them.

I was sitting near the back, but the fire burned brightly, and I was able
to see most everyone. Tonight, we had gone to the amphitheater, where there
were wooden benches built in a semicircle around the fire pit. As if we all
knew something special was coming, the mood of this campfire was already

completely different from the previous evening. The individual groups were smaller. I noticed there was a counselor next to each of the Thunderbird Five. On Friday night, a majority of the hearing impaired had huddled together in one area. The signing had been done for them by only one or two interpreters. Now, each one seemed to have paired off with their best volunteer friend. The signing would often be slower tonight, but each camper was with someone who could not only adequately express the message, but who wanted to do so for that person. In some cases, there were two volunteers sitting together, listening to Jimmy speak.

Jimmy stood behind the fire. As he spoke, the dancing flames cast his face in flickering shades of light and shadow. He began.

"I think all of us have learned a little more about friendship today, and what it means to have friends you can count on. Friends who have shared a lot with us over the years. A lot of our own best friends are right here, but at the same time, we can think of some pretty special people who are not able to be with us tonight. It makes no difference. Friendships are not limited by time or distance."

I thought of all the good friends I had known—those sitting around the campfire this night. I was smart enough to realize then that some would stick around for many years, and some would move on to other parts of the country. But the special moments of shared friendship would always remain in my memory.

Now, this was unusual. I was looking around, and everyone seemed to be paying attention. Usually, even with Jim speaking, a few would be doing their own thing, and some not so quietly. But not tonight.

"I want to talk a few moments about a very good friend of mine, someone who wants to be your friend too. He is here tonight, sitting with you around this campfire. He is a friend with whom you can share what is going on in your life. I know that each of you are a lot like me. I have many things in my life which are happy, exciting, and joyful. There are events coming up for which I can hardly wait."

~

I saw Jim George and Tammy Martin sitting together. Perhaps it was just coincidence…or was it? In less than a year, Jimmy George would call me to get her phone number. Six of us sitting around this very campfire would be in their wedding. I would have the honor of being Jimmy's best man.

Many others in attendance, though not sitting together now, would later tie the knot: John and Elise, Kathy and Bill, Grace Marie and Paul, Danae and Mike, Steve and Joy Hayes…and the list would go on.

〰

Lines on wedding invitations:

Please send an expensive gift and/or money, since you cannot attend.
—*Marianne Williams*

Be there or be square!
—*Karen Paschal*

"This friend I am talking about wants us to have those good times. He is excited when we are excited. He is there when we laugh. He wants to share those periods of joy with us and our loved ones. He wants to give us that special peace, which allows us to live those moments to the fullest. He makes us all part of one family here on earth. He was even in the car today with Elise and Lloyd, as they hot-rodded all over this camp. He cares for each of us. He allows us to care for each other."

〰

It occurred to me that so many acts of kindness were shown throughout these weekends. Some were a lot of fun, even if a little scary, like Lloyd's driving adventure. Some were not so fun. For three days, I watched Tammy Martin work with a spastic young man, who could hardly walk. However, that was a picnic compared to his problems with eating. At each meal, I also watched as Tammy ended up with almost as much food on her as the young man got down. Not a cross word was ever spoken. Just the smiles of two people working together in an attempt to make the weekend as pleasant as possible.

"He does even more. He knows when things are not going so well in our lives. He knows exactly what we are going through, and although He will not necessarily take it away, He is willing to walk the longest and roughest road with us. In fact, He will walk ahead to prepare the way."

〜

Wow! Campers and volunteers alike could relate to this message. I looked around at dozens of faces. Teenagers with smiles betrayed by a trickle of tears, which gleamed in the dancing firelight. Volunteers, a little older than children, who put aside home and personal problems to reach out to others and to try and find God's plan for their own lives. Half of my counselors came from one-parent families. Some of the others lived with daily abuse from alcoholic parents, emotional abuse from absent parents, and even sexual abuse from family members. Some were aware of these tragedies; others had, for the moment, repressed them deep into their minds.

One of my volunteers—a girl who continually showed and told campers and counselors alike how much she loved and respected them—would have given anything just to hear her father tell her that same message one time. The mother of another volunteer would spend the rest of her life in a mental institution. I saw another, whose mother was then serving a prison term. All three of these young ladies were keeping strong right arms around sightless friends, eight and nine years old.

I did not know what life would hold for each of these young ladies and their newfound friends. I did know that God loved each of them dearly, and that He sent a special friend to watch over them. I also knew that they had not let the crud in their own lives spill over into the lives of those around them, especially the campers on this retreat. If there ever was a proof that we can give to others more than we have received from those around us, it was evident in those three smiling teenagers.

Some of my best counselors had gotten involved with the Group because I was asked to do some counseling with them. I don't know if the counseling did any good, but one thing was sure true. Recruiting them for this ministry was a stroke of genius. They were all naturals at "hands-on" ministry.

I looked over at Susie Hyatt, who was in the middle of a losing battle with Hodgkin's disease. I should say *losing* only in the sense of the physical outcome. She would show us all how to be a real winner in the game of life and the fight against a terminal disease. The list could go on and on.

I saw the thirteen-year-old girl, for whom I had made a special trip to pick up. It had to be me because I was the one who had permission to check her out of the psychiatric hospital. For Tammi, however, someone very special was waiting, just beyond her line of sight this evening. It was a caring foster home, which would make all the difference in the world to Tammi's future. Tammi wrote a letter to her camp counselor and included the following poem (which was later published in her school newspaper):

Once I had a family,
A family filled with love and joy,
Like a family should.
I was just a little girl.
Times have flown by like a bird.
And as I grow older,
No longer a sweet little girl was I.
I feel a family who once loved me
Now deceived me.
No longer do they have time for me.
I feel they turned their backs on me
So I turned and walked away.
I turned from sweet flowers to sour weeds.
I fought for attention too hard,
But it seems to come out so wrong.
I thought they gave me no love
So I begged for what was not needed
To see if they cared.
They called me some names.
Now I'm gone
To another home, another family.
They bring me love, joy, and happiness.
I have learned to love them a lot.

But deep within my heart I'm torn apart.
Because I don't know who's my family
Or who will be my family.
When the warm summer days come
I just wonder, does my real family love me?
I do not know.

Perhaps, I wondered silently, *we have all learned one of life's lessons.* You do have to live each day to the fullest, try to serve God, look for ways you can bring joy into the lives of others, and, without hurting other people or your own relationship with Christ, enjoy the beauty and excitement of each new day. **Ultimately, you have to let God make some sense out of it all. You and I just need to love God, love others, and love ourselves to the best of our abilities (Matthew 22:34–40).**

"He is also there when *we* do the messing up; when it is we who hurt ourselves or someone else. You know, when we do those things that get in the way of our relationship with that special friend."

No one would ever accuse my volunteers of being perfect. In that respect, I always figured that we were somewhat like the early disciples—sometimes more trouble than we were worth. The counselors on this retreat had to contend with the same problems that beset us all: sexual frustrations and acting out; feelings of insecurity and low self-esteem; some experimenting with drugs and alcohol; spats with parents; and a continual battle with school grades. Today, looking back on things, I can see that just about the whole Group allowed Him to guide us through the tough times. Some of us, to be sure, would still struggle with and seek for that relationship, but He remains faithful and waits for us to turn back.

"The future is not always certain. However, He promises to be eternally present and, if we are His, He will make our lives count for something."

Susie and Lloyd and Peggy—they would leave an indelible mark on our lives, even though their days were numbered. I still miss them. But they were not the only ones whose lives would be cut short.

Darlene Shannabrooke and Lynne Everhart were two of the first people to help me in mission work. They went on our first retreats, which were for youth on probation. On our first retreat for girls, I gave Darlene an older-looking girl and told her to stick with her and make sure she got situated and stayed out of trouble. Five minutes later, Darlene came back and said, "Thanks a lot!" The "girl" turned out to be a young-looking probation officer. (I had met her husband, who was also a probation officer, but not her.) Darlene was one of a small group of teens, who met with me during the year to give their views and ideas on my ministry with the Peninsula Baptist Association. Illness cut her life far too short, but the quality of her life gave us all so much in that short time.

I first got to know Lynne Everhart because her parents' home was one of my hang-outs as a teenager. There was a group of us at Hampton Baptist, who used to spend a lot of evenings at the Ailors' and the Everharts'. In fact, during one period, we helped Phil Everhart, Sr., build an addition onto the house. I guess to be honest, I have to say that what we did was to go by and drink a Coke with Phil, thus allowing him to take a break. I started a tradition back then, which I carried on for over fifty years: stopping by the Everharts' and Ailors' every Christmas morning. (Now I have coffee instead of Coke. In fact, nowadays I think I live on coffee.)

Lynne was a pioneer on all our varied retreats. We ministered together on events for probation kids, foster-care teens, the handicapped, and so on. She was a "big sister" for several girls on my caseload (at the PBA). Lynne and her dog Blue were always fun to have around at these events. Several times she asked to bring a friend along because it would be a good experience for that person. Lynne was truly interested in others. She later became an elementary school teacher and a good one.

In a world of modern technology and medicine, young people still go blind. They still lose their hearing and use of their limbs. In a world of up-to-date hospitals and state-of-the-art medicine, Lynne would later die of complications at childbirth. **In a modern world of all sorts of advancements, some questionable, Lynne would leave an old-fashioned legacy of love**

and caring for others. I miss her.

Lynne once paid me what I thought was the ultimate compliment, coming from a teenager. Lucille (her mom) told me that Lynne had told her that she wanted me to be one of her pallbearers when she died. That was another unique thing about this cute blonde girl. She had a way of looking at life from different angles. For me, that it was the sentiment of a teenager, who supposedly had her whole life ahead of her, was what made that thought so special.

There was standing-room only at her funeral, and Chester Brown, our pastor, shared some of the underlined verses from her Bible. He also repeated one of my favorite Chester Brown quotes: **"We will miss her. Not because she has gone, but because she was once here."**

It was the only time I have had to wait in a line outside of a home in order to go in and talk with the parents of a loved one who was called upward. I think that was one of the real neat things about Lynne. She never made a big deal about being popular, but she was. She didn't make a big deal about doing ministry, she just did it. She didn't make a big deal about her walk with the Lord, it was just there.

I do have to tell you about the event that first endeared Lynne to me. Somewhere around her ninth birthday, our church had a picnic, at which there were several motor boats. Different groups were going out for a spin, and when it became my turn, Lynne was also in the boat. We talked and joked around. Then, trying to be funny, I pulled the oldest stunt in the book. I tied her shoelaces together.

I laughed and said to her, "What are you going to do now?"

I watched in amazement as, instead of trying to untie them, Lynne took each end and pulled them tighter together. Up until then, I had figured she was a fairly intelligent girl. She still hadn't opened her mouth to give an explanation.

So I asked, "Why did you do that?"

"So that you can't untie them," she said.

"Why would I want to do that?"

"Because when my mom sees what you have done to me, you will be in for a lot of trouble."

Took me ten minutes of hard work to get those shoestrings untied, but I knew that this Lynne Everhart was my type of girl.

~

At the amphitheater, Jim continued: "He is here right now, at this campfire. I think most, if not all of you, know who I am talking about. I am speaking of the Son of God, Jesus Christ.

"Jesus did something that would help us through all eternity. If we put our trust in Him, we will realize that He is walking beside us as we encounter the hurts and pains of our lives. When things seem to be going against us, He will give us a peace that is far greater than any 'why' we could ever ask. He will help us make the big decisions, which will shape the rest of our lives. Despite our own handicaps, He is able to help each of us find our full potential. He can help you make your part of this universe a little better. He wants to show you and me the way."

~

I was looking at a rag-tag group of volunteers, who *would* make a difference in their world. They would become youth ministers and nurses, crisis coun-selors and Christian musicians, preachers and special education teachers, Peace Corps volunteers and missionaries, school teachers and police officers; physical therapists and firefighters; veterinarians and insurance operatives, computer programmers and personnel workers. They would become deacons and Sunday School teachers, parents and volunteer youth workers, Big Broth-ers and Big Sisters, and this is to only name a few. Wes Garrett would go from leading a Baptist missionary center in Newport News to doing the same in Washington, D.C., and then later in Richmond.

Bill Sinclair would typify this group, when he took the big step of faith to go to Nashville to pursue his love of playing Christian music. He would go on overseas mission trips and play at dozens of youth camps and events. He would even come back to our area as part of a musical group brought in by Ike Newingham for a Campus Life event. In later years, he would be part of a musical group, which produced a Christmas album (*Bethlehem Morning*).

"The problem is that most of us want to hold onto both the pains and the joys in our lives. We do not want to open up and share them, on an emotional basis, with other friends or with God. Yet, that is what can make our life seem so lonely and hard.

"I think it helps us make it through the tough times when we are willing to share that burden with friends. And, of course, the biggest relief we will ever get is when we share those inner struggles and dreams with Jesus Christ, the best friend we will ever have."

〜

Every one of us around this campfire had special dreams for the future. Some of them could be easily attained; others would be harder to fulfill. One of the beneficial results of this retreat was the sharing that happened during the weekend.

Carol Gwaltney, visually impaired, and her counselor-friend Vawnetta had formed a friendship that allowed each to share with the other to an intimate degree. Theirs was a true friendship that went beyond the roles each one had on this particular night. It was a friendship based on two individuals sharing and getting to know each other. Because Carol trusted in God, she felt open to trust in her friend and share one of her own dreams. Because she told Vawnetta that she wanted to do mission work for the Lord, Vawnetta was able to pass that information on to Steve Skinner. And Steve did what he does so well:

"Mike, Carol really wants to work with us some this summer as a Smishy, and I told her we could make her a part of the team. I hope that it is all right with you." It was! Now she had a way to follow her own dream and His call.

〜

"Some of you might be wondering, can this Jesus really relate to what I am going through? Does He really care about me? Let me give you a graphic demonstration of why He knows and how much He cares for each of us here tonight. I want you all to do something. Take the nail you have and put the point in one of your palms. Now, with the other hand, push down on the nail. That's right—push down until you feel the pain, until you think it's time to stop."

It sure didn't take me long to stop pushing. I didn't even come close to drawing blood. The skin was not broken.

"The nail, there in your palm, hurt a little bit, didn't it? But probably not a whole lot. Yet, you knew you could stop anytime you chose. Most of us didn't push hard at all. Now, think back to that little bit of pain you felt before you stopped and try to imagine what it must feel like to have that same nail driven through your wrist. Imagine what it would feel like to have that nail pounded in until the blood spurts from the wound, as the nail bites into the wooden cross behind you—to feel the same hot pain coming from your ankles or feet.

"That is exactly what Jesus did for us, except the nails were larger and the pain excruciating. Yet, He was willing to allow this to be done to His body, and He did that for us—for you and me—to die for our sins. But not only that, but to point us to the life on earth we should live in His name. He loved us that much. Jesus actually earned the right to share our lives with us. He earned the right to help us through life. He earned the right to be our Lord and Savior. He loved us that much. Please bow with me for a word of prayer...."

The fire continued to bathe Jimmy's face in a mixture of hues, even as he looked down in prayer. I was transfixed by the scene around me. I was surrounded by people, some of whom cannot see or hear so well. There were volunteers and campers, who range in age from twelve to sixty. Yet every-where I looked, there were tear-stained faces. I, who always tried to remain calm and impassive in public, felt my own.

For a brief moment, I wished that I had brought my camera with me. Then I realized that it would make no difference. It wasn't the flickering firelight or small groups of friends huddling together, or even the tears that made this memorable for me. It was the moving of the Spirit of the Lord. There would be no photographs to take back, except for the most perfect picture of all. I will forever have this scene etched in my memory, and that is the way it should be.

Jimmy went on, "Now, I want you to think of something in your life that is causing you great pain—mental or physical pain. Perhaps it is something you have done to someone else, or perhaps not done. Maybe it's something that has been done to you by others, some bad experience that you have or will have to go through—something that is eating at your insides."

We had so many things we needed to turn over to the Lord. To my left was one of the prettiest girls on this retreat. She was outgoing and fun to be with. She was one of the most caring volunteers I have worked with. Yet her low self-esteem revealed itself in the guys she dated. It was an endless parade of emotionally abusive relationships. I knew that several of my volunteers were sexually seeking to find a special love. It is so amazing that we can be right in the middle of a group of people who think the world of us and still fall prey to some of the oldest lies of the devil.

I know that a few have raised eyebrows when they found out who some of my volunteers and Smishies were. And to be honest, I knew I couldn't argue with the raised eyebrows. At least not at that moment in their lives. Yet, I always felt that the youth who were my helpers on these particular activities were the ones He directed my way. Looking back on those years, I now know that despite the fact that a couple of my volunteers strayed even farther off the path, almost every one of those young people I saw around the fire would eventually make it.

I think maybe all of us there had learned one of the great lessons of the gospels. We were in need of forgiveness and acceptance—each one of us. Jesus Christ died for us, too, with all our faults and problems. He was willing to do so before we turned back to Him. He is willing to wait on each of us. And even as we are making our way back, He allows us to shine a few rays of light in the world around us.

"So often we hold onto the very thing we need to let go of. I want to challenge you to give it up to Jesus. If you are willing to step out in faith, you will find relief. True, He might not take the problem away. You could still have to face the consequences of your past actions. He does, however, promise to give us the strength to get through the valleys, and He promises to walk hand in hand with us through those valleys. He promises rest.

"Some of you are struggling with a prayer concern, which He answered in a different way than you had hoped. We need to turn those feelings over to the Lord and allow Him to show us the reasons for His answers. He will show you the course of action to take."

～

Earlier this year, Elise and Monica Holloway showed they had a better grasp of this principle than I did. Monica was a member of a non-denominational church. She and Elise had become good friends and were both in nursing school, as well as playing softball for me. At the beginning of the softball year, Monica had first met Shannon Riddle. The three had become friends. Halfway into the season, the two girls informed me that they were going to spend a week praying for a miracle—that Shannon would receive the gift of hearing. They had claimed the promise and were assuming their prayers would be answered in the affirmative. I was concerned about what might happen to their faith if the answer were no. I should not have worried about these two girls.

Sometimes, in the midst of our most fervent prayers, God grants us an unexpected miracle. Sometimes the miracle *is* in the form of physical healing. Sometimes the miracle is our own spiritual and emotional growth. Often the miracle is *in* ourselves. It was not in God's will to heal Shannon of her hearing loss. Shannon did not seem disappointed and neither did Elise nor Monica. They told me that they felt the Lord's answer was for them to simply learn more sign language and be Shannon's friends. I was glad all three were my friends, and not just because they were good ball players.

～

"If you are willing to do this, then I want you to take the piece of paper you have in your hand, and, using the nail to 'write,' put down on the paper anything you feel you should turn over to the Lord. Obviously, a nail can't really write on a piece of paper, but He will know what you have given to Him. I have talked about some of the big and painful things we need to give Him. However, this evening, perhaps you need only to give Him a decision, which will lead to something good in your life. He is interested in that as well.

"Now, please listen to me carefully. Some of you have never trusted Jesus as your Lord and Savior. If so, that decision would be the most important thing you could give to Him. If that is the case, I am praying you will do so. If you do put your trust in Him for the first time, you need to tell someone after this service is over."

Jimmy picked up the cross and looked at it for a few moments. He then laid it down on the ground in front of the fire. Next, he placed two hammers on either side of the cross. He was the first to "write" on a piece of paper. Then he picked up one of the hammers and used it to nail the paper to the cross. (This was the first time I had ever seen this kind of display, which has been used by lots of people in worship.)

"Now, as you feel led, I want you to come up and take one of the hammers. Hammer that piece of paper onto the cross. Give Him your pains and cares, your joys and dreams; trust Him to take care of anything you lay in His hands, tonight or at any time in the future. His hands you can trust!"

～

I am reminded of a poster I have at home. It shows a child holding a flower in her hands, with a quote form Martin Luther: "I HAVE HELD MANY THINGS AND LOST THEM. BUT WHATEVER I HAVE PLACED IN GOD'S HANDS, THAT I STILL POSSESS!" That is so true, and it even applies to the painful things we put in God's hands. The only difference is, in that case, what we still possess is the peace that passes understanding.

～

In awe, I sat and watched. To this day, I could not tell you who was the first or the last to walk up to that cross. Sometimes individually, sometimes in pairs or

156

small groups, we went up. At the end, I sat with empty hands. I do not know if everybody went up, but I do know that afterward, I didn't see a single stray piece of paper except those nailed to the cross. I think everyone made that short, yet long, walk to the cross that night.

⤲

"Let me give you a symbol of what Jesus will do with those things we have turned over to him this night."

Later, Jimmy told me he hadn't planned on this next course of action as part of the worship service. It just came to him that this was the appropriate thing to do. He gently laid the cross on top of the fire and stood in silence as the slips of paper began to curl up. One by one, they turned into flame and ashes. Jimmy waited till the last one had been consumed.

"The fire took those pieces of paper, and they are no more. They have vanished from this place. That's what Jesus will do for you. He will replace sin with forgiveness, fear with courage, pain with peace, and dreams with a guiding hand on your shoulder.

"Will you and I still have problems? Count on it! But also count on having access to the power that will help us overcome. If you have any questions about Jesus Christ or your relationship with Him, please do talk with me or someone else here who is a Christian. There are no Baptists or Catholics or Methodists or non-denominationalists here tonight. For we who believe, we are simply Christians. We are all serving the same Lord."

⤲

Boy, that last sentence would come home to me in a very personal way, a few years hence. Right in the middle of Steve and Terry Skinner's wedding, as I stood at the front of the church and looked around, it suddenly hit me. It was a Mennonite wedding in a Methodist church (Stel's home church) with a Southern Baptist groomsman (myself) and Bill Sinclair, the singer, who was non-denominationalist. I found myself smiling and thinking to myself, *Truly Jesus is Lord of all!*

Jim closed with a word of prayer. There was complete silence as we slowly made our way back to the cabins. Even when a couple of us came back to douse the fire, we were still quiet.

Later, of course, it became a normal, chaotic Piankatank night. This did not mean that the message had been lost on us. Rather, it showed that we realized He had really come to give us abundant life. Such an abundant life on a retreat, among friends, was supposed to have a degree of laughter and high jinks. As usual, they were not lacking on that second night.

I had one more job to do before I went to bed. I needed to move the five of us from our tent into Asia (and into the presence of Glen's snoring!), and let the five guys from that cabin move out and get a decent night's sleep. We still needed to keep a couple of the originals from that cabin with us. John Whitsel and Jimmy George agreed to be the martyrs this night.

Having done this, I hit the rack in the cabin. As I drifted off to sleep, I gave thanks to the Lord for all those on this retreat—for what they meant to each other and what they had meant to the campers for so many years.

Not a great photo of Bill on the harmonica, but it's the only one I have of Lynne Ailor at camp (in the background, to the left of Bill).

Thank you! The weekend at the camp again proved a grand success…. The majority of our trainees rarely, if ever in a lifetime, would have been able to experience the variety of activities you offered us this weekend. The exposure is not only valued for its recreational worth but for its therapeutic worth as well.

— Gail Pearsall, Supervisor of Recreation Therapy
Virginia Rehabilitation Center for the Blind

Mike,

There were so many great experiences…the exploring of shells, turtles, a black snake, rat, locating coins in a sawdust pile, the canoeing, the grand and new experience of putting on scuba gear and the challenge of using it properly, along with getting instructed one on one….

The counselors you got for us, Mike, were truly outstanding and the best, most attentive group I have worked with in a long time. They were very attentive to the individual needs of the children in short, they were great. They all gave of their time, talents and, most of all, their heart. They went hand in hand with the children, sharing and caring.

Upon our return to the Virginia School at Hampton, I noticed many of the children were busy explaining to their families some of the "stories" of camp, and many parents came up to ask if we thought we might do this again, sometime in the future. How great to see parents so genuinely interested, and all because the kids were so enthusiastic about the whole venture.

— Larry Van Wyngarden, Orientation & Mobility Specialist
Virginia School for the Deaf and Blind, Hampton

Above and below: Group pic from Camp Piankatank—Mike Saunders, Tolly Carper, Muddog, Donna Strother, Celeste Huffines, Stephanie Cantu, Kelly Williams, Deanna D'Urso, Rene Cantu, and Ellen, among others

33
Voices in the Piankatank Night

This conversation, in one of the girls' cabins, was related to me later:

Josie: "Stel, we are the only counselors still awake. One of us has to turn out the light."

Stel: "Right! I'm glad you volunteered. I'm so sleepy, I don't think I could find my way back to the bunk in the dark."

Josie: "We should have gotten bunks next to the light switch. I'm dead tired, Stel. You can make it back."

Stel: "I'll do it on the next retreat. You see better in the dark anyway."

Esther, totally blind and a veteran of many of these retreats, finally got tired of the argument. She got out of bed, feeling her way to the wall and said with a laugh, "I'll do it. I can't see on my way back regardless!"

Josie: "Great idea, Esther!"

Stel: "Esther, we love you!"

Esther turned out the lights.

~

I, being the wonderful guy I am, had moved myself into Asia with Glen and the others.

I had finally gotten to sleep before Glen let loose, but now I was awakened by the sounds of sobbing.

"What's going on?" I asked without moving.

From out of the darkness came Jimmy George's voice: "It's Howard and Edrick. They're afraid of the dark. I just woke up myself. I think they're in the same bunk now."

Whitsel, also now awake, chimed in. "They had the same problem last night, except they slept all night after they finally got to sleep. Next year, we need to bring night lights for the younger deaf kids."

I replied, "That's a really good idea, John. Jimmy, unfortunately that will be next year. You have to look after them tonight."

"What do you want me to do, sleep with them?"

"Bingo!" I said (appropriately, as that was one of Jimmy's favorite replies).

Both boys quieted down when Jimmy joined them in their shared bunk.

"Are you satisfied, Haywood? Now I probably won't get any asleep tonight!"

Sinclair quipped (was everyone awake now?), "Good! If you're awake, how about keeping Glen awake. That way the rest of us can get some sleep."

Jimmy's answer was either unintelligible or unprintable—or both!

Craig Waddell stood at the door of the cabin and asked, "Marianne, are you all descent?" Before she could answer, John Hogge, Steve Hayes, and Craig walked into the cabin. The girls had been chatting in the dark, so John Hogge turned on the light as they entered. Everyone was in their bunks, including Marianne, who had snuggled deep inside her sleeping bag.

"You all are *not* doing anything to me tonight. It took me long enough to get back last night."

"Take her! Take her!" came a muffled cry from inside one of the sleeping bags.

Craig smiled and said, "Marianne, we are not here to bug you. We like you and just wanted to see how you were doing. We figured you might like some company and—oh, no! Marianne—don't move an inch—and listen!"

Craig's voice had taken a deadly serious tone and that alone galvanized Marianne to her sleeping bag. Meanwhile, a dozen pair of eyes, even those who could not see, turned toward the top bunk in the far corner—the one in front of an open window. "Everything is going to be OK, Marianne. You are inside the sleeping bag, and it's outside. Don't anybody move. Marianne, there is a snake, lying on your bunk behind you. Must have crawled in through the window. It's down near your legs."

Despite Craig's admonition, Eurika and Ruth reached their hands slowly up toward the bunks above them, where they were met by the hands of Jeri Hudson and Kathy Smith. Even the two guys with Craig had become immobile. Except for the moving hands, Craig's voice had brought instant silence in a room of statues.

Craig reached down toward his waist with a slow, steady motion. His eyes were focused on the foot of her bunk. His voice and hand continued to operate in a slow, deliberate motion. At any outdoor camp, there is always the possibility of running into a snake. There were water moccasins in this area, although we usually found them outside in the marshy areas. Rattlesnakes were scarce, but we couldn't totally discount the possibility.

"Craig, if you are lying, I'm going to kill you!" Marianne said but still didn't move. Craig ignored her last comment. His right hand moved to chest level, clutching a large hunting knife. Marianne's eyes, now as large as saucers, were glued to the knife. Craig took a measured step forward and then stopped.

"I don't think it's poisonous, but let's not take a chance. Just everybody stay calm and quiet, especially you, Marianne."

Later, Marianne told me that she could feel the beads of sweat trickling down her cheek and her breath seemed to come in hot gulps. She was beginning to feel a slight weight at the end of her sleeping bag, and now she thought it had moved a little.

By this point, every counselor had gotten out of her bunk and was now sitting with her camper, probably hoping the camper would stay between her and the snake. At this moment, however, all movement had ceased.

John Hogge spoke in a whisper, telling Craig that he would walk across the room at an angle toward the foot of Marianne's bed. If the snake detected any motion, hopefully it would be his and not Craig's. And in that case, anything that happened would be directed away from Marianne's head. Marianne tried to pretend that she didn't hear that. John started to his right. Craig waited for John to take two steps and then he stepped toward the bunk, raising his knife above his head.

By this time, Marianne was holding her breath and hoping that something, anything, would happen in the next few seconds. Something did. John was still moving when Craig stepped quickly up to the bunk, raised his knife in his right hand, and…brought his *left hand* down hard on Marianne's leg. Her scream reverberated around the cabin. Nothing else happened and the truth suddenly dawned on her.

"Psych," said Craig in a normal voice. The three guys ducked out of the door just ahead of a dozen flying shoes.

~

Glen sat up in his bed, rubbed his eyes, and spoke loudly. "Hey, somebody! I have to take a leak!"

John Whitsel spoke up, "OK, Glen, I'm coming. I need to go, too."

"Well, I'm awake," said Troy Hicks, "and I'm about to float away, so I think I'll join you guys."

"Gee, guys, maybe we should get everybody up."

"Don't worry, Glen. You'll probably have them all awake before you get back to sleep," replied Troy, as the three of them made their way to the front porch in a semi-daze. The three studs walked to the side of the porch and, standing in a row, began to water the ground. Troy was standing in the middle of the three.

When he had finished, Troy looked to his left and asked Glen, "Are you ready to go back in yet?" He was still half asleep or he might have anticipated the next thing to happen.

Glen replied, "No, I haven't finished yet," as he made a half right turn towards Troy.

"Thanks a lot!" wailed Troy, waking up half of the cabin.

Poor Glen. If some of our trips to the bathroom seemed like an adventure, then a lot of Glen's were tragic comedy. The night before, Glen and Doug had gone to the bathroom in the middle of the night. That time they had gone to the restroom on the hill. They were walking back, Doug leading Glen, when Doug told Glen to be sure to dry his hands the next time he washed them.

He replied, "But I didn't wash my hands."

~

Greg Earwood said to Joni Hudson, who was sitting in the passenger seat of Greg's car, "Joni, I think we should have gotten to the York River Bridge by now."

Joni and Greg had left right after the campfire. They had a part in the church service the next morning, thus the late-night drive home. I had given Greg instructions, but he had not written them down. It was now 2 AM as they drove down Route 17. Joni looked ahead and breathed a sigh of relief as she saw a green sign coming into view.

"Now we can see how far we have to go. Wait a minute, Greg, it said twenty-four miles to *Fredericksburg*. Fredericksburg is in the wrong direction!" Greg hit the brakes and made a U-turn, heading back toward home. They got there at 4 AM.

~

I sat up in bed for the second time that night. My first thought was that the two deaf kids were crying again. However, nothing came from the bunk holding them and Jimmy George but the sound of deep breathing. What little light filtered in from the front door allowed me to see that Chuck Paul was also awake. When I realized what was happening, I was amazed that we two were the only people awake in the entire cabin. I also made a mental note that Glen was not the only person in the cabin who snored, though everyone else was more or less drowned out by Glen.

The only thing not drowned out by Glen's snoring was the alarm clock, which sat in the middle of the floor. It was ringing merrily away. It had not been there when we went to sleep. I was sure of that, but I still asked Chuck if he had seen anybody set an alarm.

"No, it's not one of ours. It's three o'clock! Three o'clock in the morning!" said Chuck, who showed no indication of getting out of his bunk. I must have been really sleepy because I, too, had no desire to move. I just wanted to put a pillow over my head and make the sound go away. That's what I told

Chuck.

"Well, it doesn't seem to be bothering anyone else's sleep," he ventured.

"Good point," I said, "Let's just let it ring itself out. It can't last much longer."

Chuck gave his affirmative reply by putting his head inside his sleeping bag. I followed suit. In my sleepy state, I didn't even notice that my shoes were no longer beside my bed. The clock, which had been put there by Susie Hyatt and Cindy Alba, finally wound down.

Above: Kelly Williams watches Donald go off the board, and Mike watches Kelly!

Right: Donna Hansen with one of the many volunteers who followed her around

34
Stel's Revenge

Getting to sleep on a retreat was always a major accomplishment. We just seemed to have a few added obstacles, like Freight Train Braxton. Sometimes you could get around them, and sometimes you just didn't sleep.

At the end of the previous summer, Chuck and I had been kept up till the early hours of the morning by a ten-year-old kid, who insisted there was a ghost in our cabin. And I had not even told any ghost stories. It was on our foster-care retreat. The kid had spent the whole evening jumping out from behind trees and yelling "Boo!" But at bedtime, he was petrified. No matter how many times we told him, he would not believe that the sound he was hearing in his ear was that of a mosquito flying around.

After the alarm clock at Piankatank wound down, I finally went back to sleep. It seemed like I got all of fifteen minutes worth before my own alarm went off. Luckily, this one was close enough to shut off without getting out of the bunk. I snoozed a few more minutes before deciding I really had to get up. I looked for my shoes and found them missing. Now why did that *not* surprise me. After looking around and not finding them, I put on another pair.

Then I hit the trail for my morning ritual of coffee and waking people up. This morning, I made a side trip to the flagpole to retrieve Chuck's and my shoes. They had been run up the pole by the "3 AM Alarm Clock" girls, Susie and Cindy. Shortly thereafter, everyone kind of dragged their feet into breakfast. Sundays at Camp Piankatank are kind of a repeat of Saturdays. (Hey, if it ain't broke, don't fix it; or, if these campers only get to do these activities once a year, let's give them as much time as possible to do them.)

We did start the day out with a short devotional by Jimmy George. He was actually doing a good job, and most of the campers were listening intently. One of the few who wasn't was a nine-year-old hearing-impaired kid name Jeff. He was extremely restless and seemed not to be paying much attention to his interpreter, Josie. Jimmy had no sooner finished his closing prayer, then Jeff jumped up and headed for the door. He never made it. Two paces from his chair, Jeff bent over and proceeded to throw up.

Even as he stood up, Jeff flashed a smile and said in a slow voice, "I must have drunk too much orange juice." That was Jeff's reason. The rest of us told Jimmy George that we thought there was a different cause for the problem.

The rest of the morning was beautiful, and we put it to good use, with campers and counselors spread out all over the camp, doing whatever they wanted. It was the kind of morning that made you want to be outside, enjoying life with your friends. There were even a couple of groups at the archery range again. We had lunch at noon, and then everyone hit the pool for an hour or so.

I had gone back to pack up a little before closing the pool, and when I came back to get everyone out, I was wearing shorts with my last clean pair of underpants. Admittedly, walking into the pool area was a stupid mistake. This was especially true considering the fact that Stel, whom I had been giving a hard time about the poison ivy bit, was in the vicinity. Say no more.

Stel came up from behind and gave me a push. Now, that would not have been so bad, except for the before-mentioned fact of no more clean undies, and the only clean pair of pants I had left was a brand-new, unwashed pair of jeans. Have you ever worn a pair of jeans for the first time, without undies? It is not comfortable, I will guarantee you that. Stel thought it was fun. Took me four months, but I got her back.

⌇

Stel was working at the YMCA, where I was teaching lifeguarding. I waited till one night when she came in dressed out nicely. *Has a date*, I thought. Anyway, I walked up to the service desk, where she was working with her back to me.

"Stel," I said in the sweetest voice I could muster. "I have something for you!" When she turned around, I put a handful of whipped cream in her face. It. Was. Beautiful! Both her face and my revenge.

On another occasion, she did something to me, and I threatened to get her outside her house, just before a date. It shook her up so much that she phoned her date and told him to pick her up at a neighbor's car, where she would be hiding. The best part about this one was that I didn't even get near her house. It was a bluff.

Oh, well. Back to camp. A few last-minute flurries of hugs, splashes, and fun erupted as everyone realized that the weekend was about over.

About three o'clock, I gave the bad news. It was time to head back to the cabins and finish packing. When that was done, we gathered for one last special event. Steve Skinner had one more pet he wanted to show the kids. We had purposely spaced out the exhibition of his animals because they were such a big hit with the campers, and this gave them another thing to look forward to. The pigeons had finally flown home, or at least that was where Steve said they had gone.

Left: Chicken fight! That is John Hogge in the back with Donald on his shoulders.

Above: Amy Phillips, Troy Hicks, Mike, and Bill Bowman walking away

Left and below:
Steve Skinner sharing
Alice, the black snake,
with campers

35
Alice

*A*mong Steve's other hobbies was his interests in snakes. He kept several non-poisonous ones in his bedroom at home. One of them was Alice, a six-foot black snake.

I had the greatest respect for Steve's parents. They actually let Steve and his pets abide in the same house with them. That is something I would have never done. Snakes are definitely not one of my more favorite of God's creation. In fact, I don't like being anywhere near them.

The previous spring, Steve had gotten permission to bring Alice to Campus Life to show the students after the meeting was over. He brought Alice in a cloth bag, closed at the top. He put her in a cupboard in the kitchen. The kitchen is a four-by-ten-foot space at the back of the meeting room. It has a small counter, about four feet high, between the two rooms.

After the meeting was over, I happened to be in the kitchen when Steve came in to get Alice. I backed up as close to the counter as I could. Steve reached up and pulled the cloth bag out of the cupboard. *OK*, I thought to myself, *I am going to handle this like a mature adult. I will just stand here and kind of look mildly interested as he walks by me to the main room. Just be cool.*

I was fine until Steve turned back toward me, the bag in his hand. Suddenly, the bag began to squirm. The next thing I remember is standing in the middle of the main room. Without thinking, I had vaulted over the counter and vamoosed. Steve was still standing in the kitchen, laughing. Alice was still trying to get out of the bag. I decided to go help pack up the equipment at the front of the big room.

I must admit that Alice was the most well-mannered and patient snake I have ever had the pleasure(?) of meeting. She became a regular on

171

our retreats for several years. Steve would bring her out and let those who could see get a close-up view of Alice. Then he would walk around and let the visually impaired feel her skin. All the campers were unafraid. They would eagerly pet or try to hug Alice. We even had to discourage a few from trying to kiss Alice! All the while, Alice would move slowly in Steve's hand. Most of the time she seemed to enjoy the attention. (It kind of reminded me of Steve Klem and his eels, but that's a different book.)

I let Steve run this part, and I stayed away. I didn't want anything to do with this. And I was not the only one. I have a picture of Doug Cantu trying to make Nancy Hayes touch the snake against her will. In the background is Dee Dee Hartless, whose expression would mirror mine had I been in that spot.

I want nothing to do with snakes, even on those rare occasions when my position as retreat director required me to take some action. And that reminds me of one more story.

~

In the late eighties, several new cabins were added to the camp. All of a sudden, Camp Piankatank was comfortable. There was even a new, air-conditioned cafeteria. And the cabins! They had their own bath facilities. What a luxury. No longer did we have to tramp through the night to get to the old restroom on the hill. No longer did a group of guys have reason to water the dirt off the side of a porch.

However, I figured it was kind of unfair to my new volunteers. They would never have a chance to go through such character-building experiences. They would not be able to sit around Friendly's, drinking Coke and coffee, complaining about the bathroom facilities at Piankatank. In an effort to be fair, I always offered to put the new volunteers in some of the old cabins, but they never took me up on the offer. I can't understand why....

Anyway, the first year after the new cabins had been built, I had a group of helpers from a church in Maryland. This was the group that included Kelly Ham, Audra Lamb, and their leaders, Sue and Maureen. This year was their first with us. Within a year, both of the girls would be helping to sign their church worship services. I put all of those girls in one of the new cabins with their leaders. I also felt we needed to have a couple of veterans, so I put Becky Russell and Sandy Everette in with them. (Big mistake!)

The first night of the retreat was at hand, and everything had gone perfectly. I should have known that this in itself was a bad omen. I was getting ready to hit the bed—a nice new bed in one of the nice new cabins—when I heard a knock at the front door. When I opened it, I found Becky Russell and her entire cabin standing outside.

Becky and Sue explained their dilemma. They didn't seem to think it was too big of a problem, but they did want me to take care of it. What they didn't realize was that, for me, it was a big problem, a very big problem. The problem was a large snake, which had found its way into the girls' bathroom. They didn't know how it got there, but when the first of the girls went in to get a shower, there it was coiled up in one of the stalls. She had screamed but still had the presence of mind to beat a quick retreat in the midst of her screaming.

Sue told me that she was reasonably sure it was a water moccasin, although she didn't know for certain. She had closed the door so that it couldn't get out into the main room.

I looked around me. Where was Steve Skinner when you really needed him? Not here, of course. Steve had since graduated from college and was working as a veterinarian in New York state. (Steve came back to this area and opened a practice not far from Piankatank. He has recently sold the practice, though he still works there. Steve and his wife, Terry, now have a camper and are looking for new adventures.) Up to this year, I had a bunch of guys who would have welcomed a chance to take on a water moccasin, one on one. Chuck Paul, Craig Waddell, Jim Ailor, or Bill Sinclair would have gladly taken over responsibility for this assignment. Not a single one of them was on this retreat.

"OK, OK. No problem!" I said, in what I hoped sounded like a confident voice. I started looking around for a long pole. The only thing I could lay eyes on was a broom. I picked it up and tried to look like I was formulating a battle plan. What I was really doing was trying to think up a way out and still save face! My mind was racing, but not with plans.

Thanks a lot, Lord. What am I supposed to do? I know this is probably payback for what Craig did to Marianne, but why don't you get Craig? Hey, maybe it's not a water moccasin. There are a lot of non-poisonous snakes in this area. And it may not be as big as they said. Everyone always assumes any snake is a bad one. I know I do! Do we have anyone on this retreat who knows what a water moccasin looks like? I know I should keep up on things like that, but I can never remember for sure. Is it a pointed head for poisonous, or non-poisonous? What difference does that make? I'm not about to get close enough to see its facial features. Well, I am in charge here—I have to do something....

I started toward their cabin, my trusty broom tucked under my arm. I noticed that the girls were holding back, not that I blamed them. I wanted to be back there with them. My mind was working overtime, trying to come up with something—anything!

Wait a minute! Maybe I don't have to do anything. We have an extra cabin sitting empty, and the door to the bathroom of their cabin is closed. We will be safe, as long as we keep it closed. We can leave the snake in the bathroom while getting all of their gear out of the big room. Then tomorrow, I will get the regular camp director and tell him he has a snake in one of his bathrooms. He won't mind. That's his job. But then everyone will know what a true coward I am when it comes to snakes. And these are girls.... OK, I will handle this myself! If this broom handle is long enough? How hard can this be? How big is a "big" snake?

I was so intent on my thoughts that I didn't realize what was happening when two bursts of water erupted around my feet. When the first balloon hit me in the back, I knew I had been had. I turned and stood calmly with a big smile on my face as another dozen water balloons pelted my body. I am sure that my reaction was the last thing the girls expected. All I could think of was, *Yes, there is a God!*

Left: Dee Dee Hartless, Robbie George, and Stel give three different reactions to Alice.

Below: Steve introduces Alice to campers and Jeri Hudson.

Above: Kelly Ham and Audra Lamb, our help from Maryland

Left: One of our campers heading for the top of the climbing wall

Below: Jamie Lawson helps Mario with the climbing wall.

Postscript

*T*he addition of the new cabins and cafeteria at the camp was one of two major changes in the way blind/deaf camps were run in the mid-eighties. Up until that time, I had selected each volunteer on an individual basis. There were not many youth directors who had the time or interest in helping with this particular event. In fact, there was very little other ministry to the handicapped going on in the association at that time.

Sue, from the church in Maryland, was the first youth worker to call and ask if she could bring a group down to help with the retreat. The first year, they brought seven or eight girls with them, and a good number came for each of the next several years. At the same time, the youth director at my church, Jay Russ, asked to bring a group of youth to help out. The same was true of Harald Aadahl, another youth minister. Also, four of my volunteers became youth ministers at churches in the PBA and brought volunteers in later years: Pete Smith (Menchville), Steve Burnette (Emmaus); Jimmy George (First), and Penny Jones (Buckroe). Jimmy Ailor became the senior pastor at Guilford, a church near Washington, D.C., and he also continued to come with his youth from that church. Wesley Garrett (who did so well at archery), was a member of the PBA Friendship House ministry. He later became the director of Friendship House and would bring youth from there on the retreats. Like the wrestlers from the Virginia School, some of these guys had great nicknames: Daniel Orgain ("Boo Boo"), Thomas Dickerson ("Goo"), Kenny Felton, Jerome, and Rodney. In working with our campers, they all were as good a counselor as you could get.

(The last paragraph has been put in because Jay, Harald, and several other friends told me I had to include them. I said I would. Now, it is only one paragraph, but to paraphrase Craig Waddell, "Well, I said I would include you. I never said how much!")

Anyway, things continued to move on. The Virginia School at Hampton closed down. The other state school is located in Staunton, and I didn't have contacts there. But we did continue to bring the visually impaired to Camp Piankatank. Sometimes it was for a week and at times for the weekend. Some new and unique events were added to the camp, which we made use of.

And the regular summer counselors at the camp (normally an all-male staff) continued to love me for bringing so many good-looking girls to the area for a weekend or a week. One of them fell so in love with Carol Seymore that he spent fifteen minutes cleaning the table where she and her campers were sitting after lunch. This was a counselor who had been in trouble during the summer for not cleaning tables. And it goes on and on.

I will close with a quote from Lori Blankenship, who helped so many years ago. It came in a response to a request I made of my old and current volunteers several years ago for money so that a family could get some much-needed dental care. With her check came this quote:

Well, here's to cavities and braces and beautiful teeth, geese and daffodils and Easter eggs, blue skies, springtime, timothy grass, and good friends....

And to that, I would add, "the love of God." I pass this on to all my friends, sighted and sightless, hearing and deaf, those still living and those who are now with God.

Rosetta, from the state rehab center, with her son Christopher

Epilogue

Like any event or life encounter, things tend to change. The camps for the hearing and visually impaired are one of the oldest- and longest-running ministries of my career with the Peninsula Baptist Association. We will try to keep doing this, but it won't be the same. The last link with the past is now gone.

This past year, I took a small group of counselors, and we matched up with a very small group of visually impaired. The small number did not affect the enjoyment of the day, and we even added a few additional ice-breaker games.

Rosetta Robinson came from the center in Richmond, as she had done for so many years. She arrived with her usual smile and commitment to help her teens and young adults. Rosetta and Gail Pearsall had started coming the first year it was really a retreat at Camp Piankatank. (The first two years we had done a short day's outing at Eastover.) Later, Gail moved up to another position and then got married. That took care of her retreat days.

Rosetta kept bringing her crew, and we always looked forward to seeing her. She never once complained (nor did Gail) about giving up her weekends to do this. This year turned out to be her last. She called shortly after to let me know that she would be teaching eighth grade that fall. (No one could accuse her of taking an easier position.) Her last year was special because she took her adopted son, Christopher, with her to camp. He was the same age that Howard and Edrick had been at their first camp. He is a delightful young man with a very special mother. Gail and Rosetta were two that kind of tied all the years together. (And they were so competent that you didn't read a lot about them in this book!)

New volunteers from our churches show up every year. The camps are not as large, and we began using the Eastover Retreat Center again. I wanted to mention the fact that these new volunteers are walking the same path, which so many fantastic young people have been walking for twenty-five years. And beyond the scope of this manuscript, these new young people have the same love and dedication as those who started this path with me many years ago. I wish everyone of you, wherever you might be, Godspeed, and His love in your future.

Mike Haywood
1992, 2008, 2020